The Passion of the Hausfrau

Nicole Chaison

The Passion of the Hausfrau

Motherhood, Illuminated

VILLARD V NEW YORK

Published in the United States by Villard Books,
an imprint of The Random House Publishing Group,
a division of Random House, Inc., New York.

VILLARD and VILLARD "V" CIRCLED Design are registered trademarks
of Random House, Inc.

Several of the chapters in this work originally appeared in different form in *Hausfrau Muthah-zine*.

Grateful acknowledgment is made to the Joseph Campbell Foundation (jcf.org) for permission
to reprint excerpts from *The Hero with a Thousand Faces*, third edition, by Joseph Campbell
(Novato, California: New World Press, 2008), copyright © 1949 by Bollinger Foundation,
copyright © 1968 by Princeton University Press, copyright © 2008 by the Joseph Campbell
Foundation (jcf.org). Reprinted by permission of the Joseph Campbell Foundation (jcf.org).

Library of Congress Cataloging-in-Publication Data

Chaison, Nicole.
  The passion of the hausfrau : motherhood, illuminated / Nicole Chaison.
      p.   cm.
  ISBN 978-0-345-50795-2
  1. Motherhood—Humor. I. Title.
  PN6231.M68C47 2009
  814'.6—dc22   2009008893

Printed in the United States of America on acid-free paper

www.villard.com

9 8 7 6 5 4 3 2 1

First Edition

For Craig, George, and Dora: my fellow pilgrims.
And, of course, for my mother.

hausfrau (hous' frou') *n.*
[German: *Haus*, house + *Frau*, wife] a housewife.

Contents

Part the Fourth: The Return 225

Author's Note

This book is autobiographical, but I've tinkered with some names, characters, events, details, and timelines.

All quotations on section and chapter headings are taken from Joseph Campbell's masterwork, *The Hero with a Thousand Faces,* third edition (Novato, California: New World Library, 2008), unless otherwise noted. For details, see page 235.

Introduction

HOW IT CAME TO BE
THAT i WROTE THiS BOOK

"The blunder may amount to the opening of destiny."

ne week before my thirty-ninth

birthday, my mother gave me a gift. She and my father had driven up to Maine from their house on Cape Cod to have dinner with us. After first lubricating me with her seductive and carefully chosen words, my mother handed me the gift. I didn't open it, telling her that I'd rather wait until my actual birthday.

Truth be told, I was afraid. I hadn't seen my mother in eight months. She and I have always had a stormy relationship, but it had gotten worse since I myself had become a mother. And much like the weather patterns on planet Earth, the last few years had been especially tempestuous, leaving me weak and exhausted. So I cut off communication with her, and the clime became calm and pleasant, allowing me to focus on doing some serious repair work. In other words, my therapist's couch saw a lot of my big butt. After eight months, I decided that I was in a stable enough frame of mind to have my folks up for a brief and well-orchestrated visit.

I wasn't stable enough, however, to open any gifts from my mother.

My mother's gifts tend to fall into two categories: the baffling and the provocative. Those in the latter category, which really open up my wounds, are the books. A juxtaposition of their titles suggests that my mother views my husband as a great intellect and me as a childish dimwit.

Not that I have an inferiority complex or anything. My Ivy League–educated hubby's got nothing on me when it comes to smarts. Even though Princeton University, where Craig graduated magna cum laude, has seen the likes of such luminaries as F. Scott Fitzgerald pass through its ivied halls, I can smugly boast that UConn is the alma mater of not only the Hausfrau but also Ron Palillo, who played Horshack on *Welcome Back, Kotter*.[2]

I could tell that the gift that my mother had selected to mark my thirty-ninth birthday was a book: It had that special size and heft. And earlier that evening, she'd given Craig *Team of Rivals*, the biography of Lincoln by Doris Kearns Goodwin. I could only imagine what lay in store for me.

I put the book up on the buffet, where I decided it would stay until I had the strength to open it and risk being wounded afresh. My folks went home, and the week passed. And I don't know whether it was my morbid curiosity, my propensity for torturing myself, or the fact that my mother kept calling and calling to ask if I'd opened her gift yet, but one afternoon, as I walked by the buffet, my mother's gift called out to me with a siren song. As Oscar Wilde wrote, I can resist everything except temptation. I grabbed the gift and ripped open the wrappings.

1. Answer me this: What is the sound of a daughter locked forever in ferocious struggle with the woman who gave birth to her?

2. Not to be confused with Don DeLillo, author of *White Noise* and *Libra*.

3. For the love of God, will somebody please explain to me what these are?

And this is what I saw:

OK. So I need to give a little background. "Romo" (aka Bill Romanowski) was this guy I had gone to high school with back in the early 1980s. He dated and in fact deflowered one of my closest friends and stood around the same kegs o' beer I did, out on the dirt roads near our hometown. I remember him as a heart-throbby, grinning jock who never took off his letter-man's jacket.

And get this: Sophomore year in high school, I was a cheerleader for Rockville High's boy's basketball team. Bill Romanowski was a three-season athlete and played basketball. I did a special cheer for him that went a little something like this:

> Cheer for Romanowski!
> Let's go!
> Yay, Billy! Yay, Romanowski!
> Yay, rah rah for Billy Romanowski!

Yes, I participated in an extracurricular activity in which I jumped around, cheering for the opposite gen-der's accomplishments on the basketball court. I also danced in a halftime routine to "Our Lips Are Sealed" by the Go-Go's. And as if that wasn't humiliating enough, our coach forced us to weigh in every week in front of the entire squad, and if we gained more than two pounds during the season, we'd get kicked off the team. Ah, the eighties!

---

4. To achieve "tubes": Part wet hair down middle and blow-dry with small round brush into "tubes." Enhance the tube-ness of the "tubes" with sizzling-hot curling iron. Spray with three applications of Aqua Net.

Billy went on to play football for Boston College and then was drafted into the NFL. His career[6] included five Super Bowls, lots of concussions, and some rather unsavory behavior.[7] But in the 1990s, while Billy's star was rising, he was Vernon, Connecticut's favorite son. Parades were thrown in his honor. Bill Romanowski Day was declared. I'd moved to Boston by that time, but my parents kept me up on Billy's accomplishments. And it really irked me that the pinnacle of fame in my hometown was reached by a linebacker. As I struggled to pay the rent each month by patching together freelance writing gigs, Billy was raking in so much dough that he was able to finance the creation of a high-tech athletic facility and nighttime playing field at our old high school. While I ate ramen noodles and stayed up all night writing short stories, Billy was jetting to Hawaii and partying with the likes of Adam Sandler. When my parents told me the news of Billy's triumphs, I filed the info away resentfully and fantasized about eclipsing his star one day with some award-winning prose.

---

5. George always asks the tough questions.

6. San Francisco 49ers (1988–1993); Philadelphia Eagles (1994–1995); Denver Broncos (1996–2001); Oakland Raiders (2002–2003). Highlights: Played 243 consecutive games, an NFL record among linebackers. Won four Super Bowls; is the only linebacker to start in five.

7. Brawled with teammates during a 49ers practice session (1989). Ejected from a game and fined $4,500 for kicking a running back in the head (1995). Fined $20,000 for breaking the jaw of a quarterback; twisted the testicles and spat in the face of a wide receiver (1997). Fined $42,500 for three illegal hits plus a punch thrown at a tight end (1999). During a practice with the Oakland Raiders in 2003, punched a teammate in the face, breaking his eye socket and forcing the player to retire; had to pay $340,000 in compensatory damages (2005). Openly admitted to using steroids on *60 Minutes* (2005).

OK. So now flash forward to a few days before my thirty-ninth birthday—when I finally opened my mother's gift and discovered the treasure that is *Romo: My Life on the Edge: Living Dreams and Slaying Dragons* by Bill Romanowski with Adam Schefter and Phil Towle.[8] The book stirred up all sorts of muck that I had deluded myself into thinking I had resolved in therapy. Instead of interpreting my mother's gift as a joke, I let it give me a serious psychic ouchie. And like a raving lunatic, I told anyone who would listen about what my mother had done.

It was in the dramatic retelling to our friends Jake and Leah over dinner one night at our house that I slowly began to move through my ego-driven rantings. Jake had been a football fan since he was a kid and knew all about Romo and his career. Leah knew nothing whatsoever about football. Together, their insights prompted me to crack open the cover and take a peek inside.

I had never actually considered reading the book, such an affront it was to all things well considered and eloquently stated. But that evening, once Jake and Leah and their kids had gone and our kids were asleep, I began reading *Romo: My Life on the Edge: Living Dreams and Slaying Dragons* by Bill Romanowski with Adam Schefter and Phil Towle—a book that would change the course of my destiny.

However, at first its lessons were lost on me—so caught up was I in spotting the myriad grammatical errors and also obsessively comparing the trajectory of Bill Romanowski's life with my own, detail by painful detail (as follows).

8. Apparently, Romo needed both a ghostwriter (Adam Schefter) and a life coach (Phil Towle) to help him craft his story.

ROMO!

DRUGS OF CHOICE

steroids

ibuprofen phentermine

JULIE 'N' ROMO
IN SPORTS ILLUSTRATED

CAR OF CHOICE

SEAN PENN

1988: While Romo was a rookie for the 49ers, his first trainer interrupted the game film they were watching and shouted, "Romo! If I ever see anybody push you in the back and you don't do something about it, I will personally kick your ass!"

1989: Romo writes, of discovering phentermine, an appetite suppressant with amphetamine-like effects: "What phentermine did for me was put me in the zone. I truly wanted to run into a brick wall as hard as I could. You cannot believe how good it felt to hit somebody. It was like, give me more of this, give me more of the hitting, give me more of the pain."

1993: Romo marries a "knockout brunette" named Julie. He writes: "We fit together like San and Francisco." See rendering at left, from a *Sports Illustrated* shoot; note the taut abdomens and ripped biceps.

1999: By this time, Romo and Julie have two children: a six-year-old boy and a two-year-old girl. Romo describes his favorite sound in the whole wide world thusly: "To me, [someone moaning at the bottom of a pile of football players] is a sound as sweet as ocean waves. There's nothing better than knocking somebody out, seeing them struggle to get up, and watching a stretcher brought out to carry them off."

After his fourth Super Bowl win, Romo and Julie got to pick out a new car of their choice: "Julie fell for a fully loaded black Mercedes SL600 convertible with a V12 engine, one of the rarest models in the country. [We] drove off the lot in the $138,000 car."

Romo suffered dozens of conscussions in his lengthy career, and bodily punishment begins to take its toll. He loses his senses of smell and taste and suffers from memory loss.

2004: Romo goes to Hollywood, landing a part in Adam Sandler's remake of *The Longest Yard*. Later that year, Romo bumps into Sean Penn in a New Orleans hotel lobby: "We spent the next seven hours, into the early morning, talking about improving relationships and growing and changing as a person."

1988: During a critique of one of the Hausfrau's short stories in a fiction-writing workshop, the instructor remarked: "I want to know what's at stake in this story. I mean, do you really *earn* that ending?"

1989: Drinking three to four dark-roast coffees a day, the Hausfrau begins her love affair with the little brown bean. She comments, "After some coffee and a cigarette, I was like, give me more of the typing, give me more of the writing, give me more of the pain."

1993: The Hausfrau marries high school English teacher Craig Lapine and moves to Ohio to pursue a master's degree in writing. She muses: "We fit together like Cleve and Land." Note the Hausfrau's baggy T-shirt and men's boxers, which cleverly conceal the flab that lies beneath.

1999: By this time, the Hausfrau and her hubby have one son, George, who is two. He is the light of his parents' eyes and also what some describe as "high-need" or "spirited." The Hausfrau has two favorite sounds: the glug-glug of a bottle of good wine being poured into a glass circa 6:00 p.m., and, more rarely, her hubby stating: "You sit. I'll deal with the boy."

2004: After birthing two babies, the Hausfrau says bye-bye to vaginal tone and continence while sneezing, running, or jumping on a trampoline.

It really ticked me off that Bill Romanowski got to hang out with Sean Penn all night while I had been loving him since he played Jeff Spicoli in *Fast Times at Ridgemont High*—a movie I watched obsessively at my friend Marney's house in 1984—because she had a VCR and we could rewind and replay the Sean Penn scenes over and over again and fast-forward through the Phoebe Cates scenes. Marney and I never tired of Sean's crooked grin, his pot-smokey voice, his knobby-kneed saunter, or the way he delivered one of my favorite lines in all of cinematic history: "Aloha, Mr. Hand!"

I fantasized about what it would be like if I got to hang out with Sean Penn for seven hours, and I won't record that fantasy here, but rather will depict a more pragmatic account of what would probably happen if I were to bump into my favorite celebrity in a hotel lobby. Two different scenarios jump to mind.

Sean! Sean Penn! Hi! I can't tell you what a pleasure it is to meet you! I've long admired your integrity as both a human being and an actor. And your range—your versatility—is incredible! From falling out of a pot-smoke-filled surfer van in "Fast Times at Ridgemont High" to your portrayal of disturbed murderer Matthew Poncelet in "Dead Man Walking" ... Though I admit to being underwhelmed by "The Crossing Guard," the rest of your work has kept me riveted! And I wonder: What was it like being married to Madonna? Did you ever see her go to the bathroom?

9. Like the time back in the eighties when my friend John Vlahides and I got to meet Andy Warhol at the Palladium in New York City, and all I could think to say to him was, "I like your wig." Jesus.

10. And wholly dependent upon drinking several glasses of wine beforehand to lube myself up.

11. Eerily mirroring my mother's words from page 3.

And so I absolutely seethed with jealousy, and as usual, my hubby, Craig, bore the brunt of my cuckoo rantings, which I unleashed on him in a fit of righteous indignation. I began to believe that my mother's words, repeated in my Sean Penn fantasy, were true: I *did* need serious help. Why was I begrudging Romo his fame and fortune? Oh, wait. I know why.

After sinking into a quagmire of self-pity and insecurity—which I hope was a midlife crisis, because I'd like to get that one out of the way and get on with the second half of my life—the dust began to settle and I started to do some soul-searching. I was disparaging Romo's special calling and his book because *I* felt insecure about *myself*. Sure, Romo had spent the last twenty years ramming his head into the torsos of other men, but at least he had put himself out there. I, on the other hand, had always wanted to write a book but had never actually done it. And I hadn't written my own book because I had been afraid. I was afraid that my book would suck. Or that no one would read it. Or that people would read it and hate it. I was a big wuss!

But I would be a big wuss no more! I decided then and there to stop making excuses for myself and get down to some serious work.

I think it was Romo himself who put it best in his lyrical masterwork—*Romo: My Life on the Edge: Living Dreams and Slaying Dragons* by Bill Romanowski with Adam Schefter and Phil Towle—when he "wrote":

I recognize now, though, that I've become my most important obstacle to happiness and fulfillment. I'm my own biggest dragon. Aren't we all?

And my answer to that is yes, Romo. We are. We certainly are.

Part the First

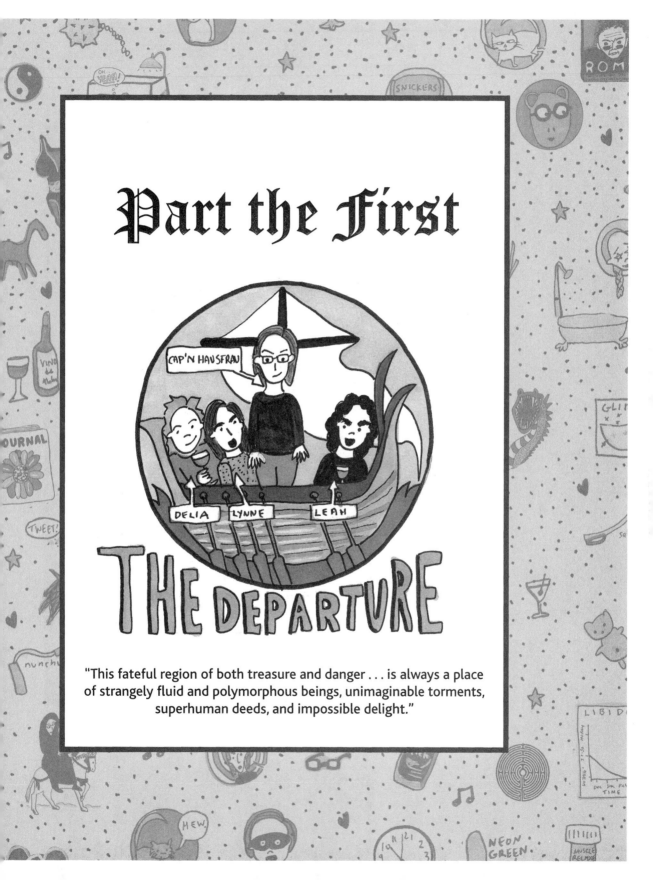

THE DEPARTURE

"This fateful region of both treasure and danger . . . is always a place of strangely fluid and polymorphous beings, unimaginable torments, superhuman deeds, and impossible delight."

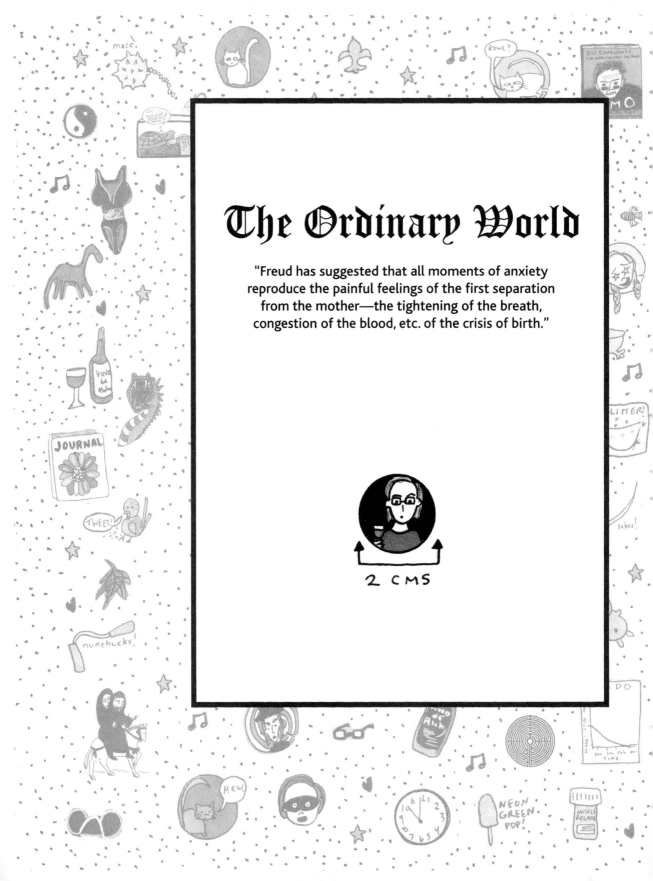

The Ordinary World

"Freud has suggested that all moments of anxiety reproduce the painful feelings of the first separation from the mother—the tightening of the breath, congestion of the blood, etc. of the crisis of birth."

2 CMS

Another Friday Night Shabbat Party

t was the following Friday night, during a Shabbat[1] celebration at Jake and Leah's house, during which the vino took center stage and the challah lay forgotten, that I recounted my pathetic attempts to write my book to the adults assembled there.

The children—and there were many—proved to be adaptable and quit asking about the Shabbat rituals (such as lighting candles and smothering butter on challah) and instead began racing over the wooden floors in the PlasmaCar and throwing popcorn (i.e., dinner) at each other.

Others have spoken of the blank page as a vast white expanse, but when I had sat down earlier that week at the computer to begin work on my book, it had seemed more like the gaping maw of a she-beast. What the hell did I have to write about? I had been at home, after all, for the past ten years, raising the kids and keeping the house together. You might say that my scope had narrowed somewhat, and now here I was, drinking too much wine and complaining loudly to my husband and friends about the fact that a brain-damaged jock I knew in high school had published a book but I had nada.

---

1. The Jewish Sabbath, which begins at sundown on Friday and ends at sundown on Saturday and is traditionally celebrated by gathering with friends and family and lighting candles, saying blessings, breaking bread (called challah), and drinking wine and then sharing a festive meal, usually involving chicken.

HAUSFRAURANT

THIS WHOLE ROMO BOOK THING HAS REALLY PUSHED ME OVER THE EDGE. I'VE BEEN TRYING TO SIT DOWN AND WRITE ALL WEEK — BUT IT'S SO PATHETIC! I SIT THERE, STARING AT THE COMPUTER SCREEN — MY MIND TOTALLY BLANK — AS IF ALL MY THOUGHTS AND IDEAS HAD GOTTEN SUCKED OUT OF MY BRAIN BY A GIANT VACUUM CLEANER. IT'S LIKE I HAVE NOTHING TO SHOW FOR THE LAST TEN YEARS OF MY LIFE!

MY FATHER ALWAYS SAYS "MOST MEN LEAD LIVES OF QUIET DESPERATION" — HE STOLE THAT FROM THOREAU OR SOMEONE — BUT WHAT ABOUT US HAUSFRAUS? WHAT ABOUT OUR QUIET DESPERA- TION? WHAT ABOUT OUR STORY? WE DON'T HAVE ONE! AND YOU KNOW WHY? BE- CAUSE WE'RE TOO BUSY WIPING BUTTS AND MAKING DINNER AND FOLDING LAUNDRY AND SWEEPING UP CHEERIOS AND WORRYING ABOUT THE PLANET AND MAKING DENTIST APPOINT- MENTS AND PICKING UP AND ORGANIZING OTHER PEOPLE'S CRAP TO BE ABLE TO COGITATE ON THE VERITIES + COMMIT IT TO PAPER!

AMEN, SISTER!

HOGGING THE BUTT

After a while, the PlasmaCar began to lose its allure, and so the girls went into the playroom to rehearse a play they were working on about a family of mermaids. George rallied his troops to attack the mermaid-thespians. The men sat down and drank beer. And we ladies retired to the back porch to share some wine and a clandestine cigarette.

I complained bitterly to Lynne, Delia, and Leah about my attempts at writing that week—about how I'd sat and stared at the she-beast-screen for what seemed like hours and then I'd pecked out a few words and then deleted them. About how the only thing I'd re-ally written in the last ten years was the journal that I started keeping after Dora was born—just snippets of stories and sketches. About how I'd decided I wanted to write a *real* hero's journey, and thus beat Romo—kick his ass, really—and so I'd gone to our bookshelf and looked at the great works of Western literature and no-ticed how they were all written by men about men's journeys. I ranted on about how, in true hausfrau fash-ion, I'd turned my anger to good use by cleaning the en-tire house and washing all the floors and finally doing all the laundry—but before I knew it, here we were, at another Friday night Shabbat party, and a whole week had passed and I hadn't written a word.

Of course, my friends immediately rallied around me, sharing nuggets of encouragement—Lynne giving me a bona fide pep talk—but I had drunk way too much wine and the cigarette was starting to make me feel sick, and really, I was in such a funk that I couldn't hear anything my friends were trying to tell me.

So instead of doing any real listening or introspection, I changed the subject and asked Leah how her week had been. Leah is a midwife and is on call a lot and works several days in a row delivering babies with no sleep and then comes home to take care of her kids and hubby and house. She astounds me! I have no idea how she does it! I bow down to her.

Leah told us that for some reason the week had been really intense for her, delivering babies, and that the births all ended up going well but that they were long and drawn out, one even lasting three days and nights. She said she was so tired at one point that she started having some interesting thoughts and got introspective about birth as a metaphor and had a major revelation about the birthing process, which she shared with us and which really blew my mind.

Then we started talking about our own birth stories, but just as Delia was in the middle of hers, Craig poked his head out of the sliding glass door and told

THE RANT CONTINUES

SO THEN I GO TO THE BOOKSHELF FOR INSPIRATION, AND BECAUSE CRAIG AND I WERE BOTH ENGLISH MAJORS, WE HAVE ALL THE CLASSICS—AND I'M STANDING THERE LOOKING, AND ALL THE BOOKS ARE HERO'S JOURNEYS—BUT THEY'RE ALL BY MEN, ABOUT MEN: GOING TO WAR, KILLING STUFF, GETTING CRUCIFIED, ETC. AND WHAT I WANNA KNOW IS WHAT ABOUT US? WHERE'S MY STORY? I PUSHED BABIES OUT OF MY VAGINA FOR GOD'S SAKE! DOESN'T THAT DESERVE A MENTION IN THE WESTERN LITERARY CANON?

STILL MONO-POLIZING THE CIGARETTE

RIGHT ON, MAMA

I DUNNO. I THINK YOU TOTALLY CAN WRITE THAT STORY. I THINK IT WOULD BE A REALLY GOOD ONE. THE LAST TIME YOU SHOWED ME YOUR JOURNAL AND I READ ONE OF YOUR STORIES, I LAUGHED SO HARD THAT I PEED A LITTLE. WHY DON'T YOU JUST TAKE YOUR JOURNAL AND MAKE A BOOK OUT OF ALL THE STORIES IN IT?

LYNNE'S PEP TALK

us that the kids were melting down and that we should definitely go.

Extracting the children from Leah and Jake's house was an ordeal that took forty-five minutes of shouting and procrastination, which I fueled, as I was having trouble pulling myself away from my girlfriends. I didn't want to go home at all but wanted to stay up late into the night talking and sharing birth stories—except that I was starting to feel sick: woozy and unstable on my feet and incredibly tired.

Once we got into the car, the bickering started. I left the discipline up to Craig, who was at the helm of our Subaru Forester, because I was having trouble coping— I felt so strange, not just intoxicated but strange. I was sweating, and I think I was feverish, although Craig felt my forehead and said no, I was just clammy. The car was spinning, and it was all I could do to keep it together for the two-mile drive back to our house.

When we got home, climbing up the stairs to the second floor of our house took every ounce of my energy. My legs were numb and heavy and my head kept spinning. Craig corralled the kids right up to bed, and I shut the lights out and turned the computer off, pausing only for a moment to watch the glowing she-beast, who seemed to growl and smile at me tauntingly before being clicked off into beastly slumberland.

Upstairs, I hugged and kissed the kids and said goodnight before collapsing into bed, too exhausted even to brush my teeth. I fell asleep immediately, and was awoken at some point by Craig, who was shaking my arm and telling me to be quiet. He said I must have been having a nightmare because I kept yelling incomprehensibly.

I was completely disoriented and was running a high fever by this time. I don't know how high, because our thermometer had recently been destroyed—I had needed it when Dora had had strep throat a few weeks earlier, but couldn't find it, only to later discover it in the turtle tank, covered with algae.

The Passion of the Hausfrau 21

Aspiration

he next morning, I awoke with a wretched case of pneumonia. As I fought the infection in my lungs, my fever raged and made me sweat so much that I completely drenched my pajamas and sheets. I coughed and coughed and scared the crap out of myself and the kids. When I succumbed to a particularly bad coughing fit, my body would lurch forward to unleash the sputum, and I would hark and hark and then I would just about cough my lungs right out of my chest—but instead, I'd pee in my pants![1]

I lay in bed, quarantined and delirious, in a pool of my own fluids, the bed around me littered with sputum-rife Kleenex and plenty of reading materials I'd taken off the bookshelf.[3]

It made perfect sense that I'd developed pneumonia. The lungs are a particularly loaded organ for the women in my family; I'd had bronchitis perpetually as a child and had gotten pneumonia twice already since becoming a mother. My mother's mother, Mildred (aka Grammy Mil), whom I absolutely adored, was a

---

1. One of the perks of carrying babies around in utero for nine months is that whenever I laugh or cough or run or jump, I piss myself silly.

2. I'm not reciting Shakespeare here, folks! This is how my cough sounded.

3. You know, the classics: Joseph Campbell's *The Hero with a Thousand Faces,* Chaucer's *Canterbury Tales,* Dante's *The Divine Comedy,* and *Romo: My Life on the Edge: Living Dreams and Slaying Dragons* by Bill Romanowski with Adam Schefter and Phil Towle. Also with me were my journal and some back issues of *The New Yorker.*

three-pack-a-day smoker for sixty years. Strong as an ox, she ate and drank and smoked to excess—usually simultaneously. She died of complications from pneumonia the year George was born.

My mother had also developed pneumonia several times and had smoked like a chimney until she was forced to quit when she developed a mass in her lungs. My earliest childhood memories involve lying down in the back of our Volkswagen, my nose pressed to the pleather seat, trying to smell something other than cigarette smoke.

And I had smoked, too, for years and years before I had the kids. I smoked a lot while I was writing, which was most of the time, before I got pregnant, and then I quit. I stopped writing and smoking at the same time—just like that.

But the night before at Jake and Leah's, I had smoked with the ladies on the back porch. I could still taste the cigarette in the back of my throat, which made me launch into another coughing fit.

The phone rang. It was my mother, wondering if I had opened my birthday present yet.

4. Refuses to commit to memory the fact that my doctor is a woman.

I told her that yes, I had, but that my aspirations[5] for my fortieth year on the planet had shifted somewhat, and presently I was focusing on trying to breathe without coughing my lungs up whilst urinating in my undergarments.

I asked my mother if she could come up and help us—maybe make a few meals, watch the kids so Craig could get some work done, etc.—since I was sure I'd be bedridden for a while. But my mother explained that she was going to be busy at the Edward Gorey House in Cape Cod.[6]

"I wish there was something I could do to help," my mother said, before we hung up.

I coughed and coughed and peed a little and then I called Leah. She said I'd probably need antibiotics but that she could advise me about some herbs that could help heal my messed-up lungs. She told me not to worry, that I was probably going through a transformation, and that coughing up all the yuck in my lungs was the beginning of the journey.

Leah gave me the names of some herbs that she wanted me to make into an infusion and drink.

5. Interesting, isn't it, that the word "aspiration" means "a strong desire to achieve something great" and also "the act of breathing." Was there a connection between my frustrated literary dreams and my bout of pneumonia?

6. My mother volunteers as a tour guide at the Edward Gorey House in Yarmouth Port, Massachusetts, where my parents retired the same year that George was born. We went on one of her tours once—but that is a story for later. See page 208 if you can't wait.

I asked Craig if he would go to Whole Foods to get the herbs, and then I fell into a restless and feverish sleep. Later, Craig and the kids brought me the infusion. It tasted god-awful, but I managed to choke it down.

And soon after, everything got strange and confluent and squiggly. Was I hallucinating? Was it the fever? Was it those herbs? I cannot say for sure. What I do remember is that my bed became hard as wood and morphed into the planks of the deck of a ship. And I was like Max in that book *Where the Wild Things Are*. And then I was the figurehead at the prow of an ancient ship. And then I was at the helm, like Odysseus, sailing between Scylla and Charybdis.

The Call to Adventure

"The call to adventure signifies that destiny has summoned the hero and transferred his spiritual center of gravity from within the pale of his society to a zone unknown. . . . For those who have not refused the call, the first encounter of the hero journey is with a protective figure (often a little old crone) . . . who provides the adventurer with amulets against the dragon forces he is about to pass."

4 CENTIMETERS

B.C.
(Before Children)

In the beginning,

the house was quiet. Indeed, there was no house at all. There was only a small apartment outside Boston, Massachusetts.

In that small apartment, it was a time unlike now. It was a time when my brain was able to produce measurable amounts of serotonin. It was a time when I had enough cognition and free time to finish crossword puzzles. It was a time when my vagina had structural integrity.

It was a time when I knew nothing but thought I knew it all. It was a time when I judged other folks mercilessly (OK—I still do that) but had about as much introspection as a mosquito. It was a time when I could go out for brunch. Swear with abandon. Urinate in privacy.

It was a time Before Children.

And I was a freelance writer and my hubby, Craig, was a graduate student. We lay around on Sunday mornings, eating bagels and drinking coffee and reading *The New York Times*—he the social pages and I the Book Review—and having sex.

And then I got pregnant.

nward now, eight months, to
Ledyard, Connecticut, where I went to wait out the
end of my pregnancy at Grammy Mil's house while
Craig prepared for his final exams. Having gained sixty
pounds during the pregnancy, I was huge and ultra-
sensitive and craved the comfort and familiarity of my
grandmother and her ancient couch.[1]

Oh, Grammy Mil! I miss her so! She was a bona fide
eccentric, who drove a Porsche 911 Targa with a lead
foot, chain-smoked More cigarettes, drank White
Russians, and could recite long passages from Walt
Whitman's *Leaves of Grass*—her favorite book—from
memory. Her house was a dark, smoke-filled, prefab
cave, which housed the few precious antiques she'd
managed to drag out of the flames when the farmhouse
burned to the ground twenty years before, when my
grandfather, George, was still alive.

Also living at Grammy Mil's house at that point was
her youngest son, my uncle Phil, who had recently gotten divorced and—at middle age—had returned to the

---

1. Ledyard, Connecticut, is also the home of Foxwoods Casino, which
abutted Milly's hundred-acre farm and white pine forest like a mirage.

2. This honker of a diamond ring was so unbelievably large and garish that when thieves broke into her home and stole her jewelry box, they
threw the ring into the bushes in front of her house, thinking (I imagine)
that it was a giant fake, like the kind you'd get out of a bubble-gum machine.

family manse for pretty much the same reason I was there: to take comfort in Milly. The difference was that, whereas I wanted to sit on the couch while my grandmother held court from her throne, Phil preferred surfing for porn on the Internet and going out back to shoot guns at the hundreds of empty vodka bottles he'd amassed over the past year.

My mother called several times each day, not to talk, per se, but to inquire about what I was doing and also what her brother and mother were doing and what we were eating. It was unclear what exactly my mother was concerned about. I had told her that I was visiting Grammy Mil to put in a perennial flower bed—since Milly loved gardens but her arthritis prevented her from digging in the dirt. This had seemed like an acceptable explanation to my mother when I first told her about my plans, but now she seemed suspicious and worried.

The real reason I was there was because I wanted to connect with my grandmother. I loved to sit on her couch and listen as she told stories about her life—the same stories over and over again, with the same one-liners at the end, as familiar and predictable to me as the way she would sharpen her carving knives before slicing up her succulent Thanksgiving turkey or Easter ham: by dragging the long blades back and forth against each other while the rest of us sat at the table, salivating like Pavlov's dogs.

The story that fascinated me most was the one Milly told about why she had suddenly stopped painting. She had been a talented oil painter and had studied her craft at Pratt Institute in Brooklyn before she met my grandfather and got married and started having babies. My grandfather traveled all the time for his job and was only home a few weekends a month. My grandparents also moved around a lot to accommodate my grandfather's job, and so it became difficult for Milly to form a community to support her as she raised three children.

I loved to paint so much that when I started having my babies, I had to stop altogether. I tried to paint a few times after your mother was born, but I scared myself silly one day when your mother was just a li'l babe. I was itching to paint one morning—it had been years since I'd picked up a brush—so I put your mother in the playpen in the living room and went to the back of the house to paint for a while. The next thing I knew, I looked at the clock and five hours had slipped by, with me completely unaware of a thing except for the painting. And when I went into the living room, there was your mother, hungry and with a horribly dirty diaper. She'd been crying—but I didn't know for how long because I hadn't even heard her. It scared me so much that I put my paints away and never took them out again.[3]

3. I felt bad for my mother! I imagined her there, hungry and all alone, in a festering diaper, crying for her mother.

Grammy Mil started painting again in her eighties—beautiful, vivid floral still lifes, which she had framed and gave away as gifts for birthdays and at Christmas. And at the end of my visit with her B.C., she handed me a blank journal that she had painted with a bright sunflower—a burst of gold and green on the cover. Inside, she'd inscribed the first page with the following quote from Walt Whitman's "Song of Myself":

Smile O voluptuous cool-breath'd earth!
Earth of the slumbering and liquid trees!
. . . Prodigal, you have given me love—
Therefore, I to you give love!
O unspeakable passionate love!

I hugged and kissed her good-bye and drove back to Boston, weeping and having Braxton Hicks contractions all the way.

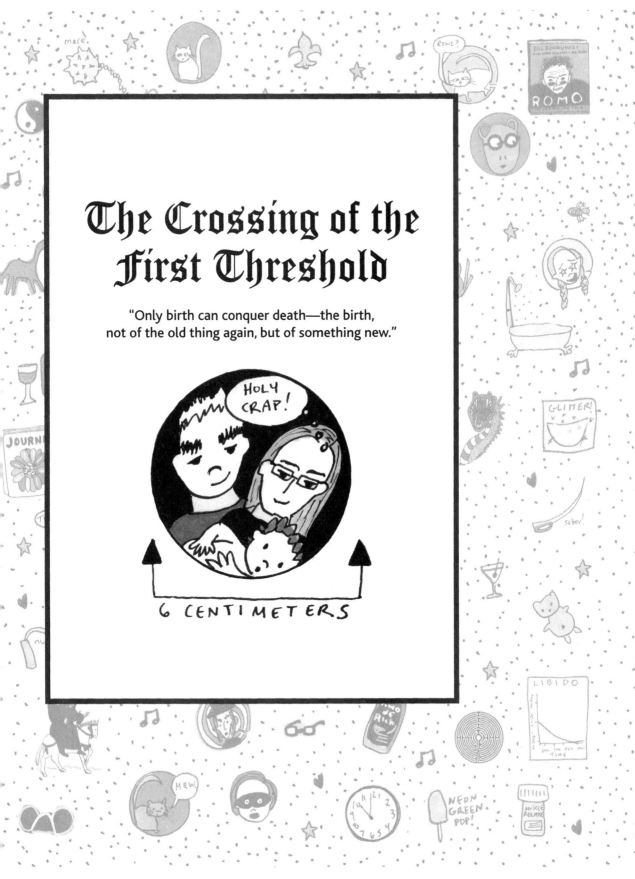

The Crossing of the First Threshold

"Only birth can conquer death—the birth,
not of the old thing again, but of something new."

How It Came to Be that I Gave Birth in a Hospital Utility Closet

uring the birth of our first child, I found myself plunged into a heroic odyssey, one in which my cervix stretched open wide enough to accommodate the head of another human being. My nether regions bulged out like the muscles of a comic book hero, which I noticed when the nurse held up a mirror so I could see my son's head emerging.

It was your typical, run-of-the-mill American birthing scenario: Craig and I had arrived at the hospital—I, projectile vomiting from the squeezing excruciation in my lower abdomen; he, clutching my arm and anxiously pleading for assistance from the woman at the admitting desk. Because the hospital was at that moment out of birthing rooms, we were quickly ushered into a utility closet, and a gurney was pulled in for me to labor upon. The nurse hooked me up to a fetal monitor and an IV drip and then left me with my hubby to suffer wave upon wave of bodily agony.

At some point, the nurse came back and put her gloved fingers inside me and said, "Ten centimeters! Time to push!"

INSIDE THE

MY PERSPECT-
IVE ON OUR
"BIRTHING SUITE"

WHO ARE
THESE PEOPLE
? ? ? ? ? ? ?

LOOK!

AAAAAAH!

UTILITY CLOSET

Just then, several strangers—whom the nurse cursorily introduced as "residents"—entered the utility closet. She asked if we minded if they watched the birth. I was unable to answer.

Someone clicked on what appeared to be a searchlight and aimed it at my crotch. Two of the strangers grabbed my legs and held them aloft, while Craig pushed against my back. An oxygen mask was slapped onto my face. I tore it off and threw it on the floor.

"Push!" someone yelled.

And I would not describe what my body did just then as a "push."[1] Rather, I completely surrendered to my uterus's need to violently wrench the baby inside of me out into the waiting world, while I lurched forward and bore down again and again against the explosion of searing pain in my perineum, as if possessed.

I think that I was possessed. Indeed, when the nurse leaned forward and held up the mirror so I could see the baby crowning, I snarled at her like Regan in *The Exorcist*. I was sure I was about to rip open. I thought I would die. And I did.

I was reborn as the Hausfrau.

---

1. Maybe it's just me, but in this situation, I need to report that "push" is to "childbirth" as "wiggle" is to "convulsion."

The Birth of Hausfrau

ver the next few hours, the next few weeks, the next few months, the next few years, I experienced a love affair unlike any other.

I was completely unprepared for it, for the depth of emotion I felt for this tiny boy, our son, whom we named George after my grandfather, Mildred's husband. I'd never read about this kind of love, or seen anything like it on TV or in the movies.

Such a sweet blur of nursings, oglings, diaperings, sleep deprivation, gift opening, baths, and photo ops! I moved through it all in a haze of love. I existed only to provide comfort and nourishment for my baby. His cries were like daggers in my heart. His satisfaction was my ecstasy. Everything else dropped away.

A.D.
(After Dilation)

"After our son was out of my body and the endorphins wore off, the comedy in mothering came into focus. I felt like a comic book hero: Every moment unfurled like a psychedelic journey into the maw of some dark and hilarious new beast."

—The Hausfrau, a journal entry

8 CENTIMETERS

How It Came to Be that I Gave Birth in a Cattle Trough

And now, flash forward four years, almost to the day—when the story really starts to get good 'n' juicy. In the interim, we'd moved to Portland, Maine, and bought a three-story fixer-upper Victorian. I was now hugely pregnant and sitting on the couch with George, who was wearing his Batman costume and watching *Arthur* on PBS. Craig was nailing down floorboards in the upstairs hallway.

I had just gotten off the phone with my mother, who had called to register her concerns about home birth. Craig and I had made the decision to have this next baby at home, in the comfort of a birthing tub.[1] After all, I had given birth to George in a hospital utility closet in front of complete strangers. If I could do that, then I could certainly have this baby in a nice warm tub of water in the privacy of our bedroom, with the help of a trusted midwife.

Suddenly, I felt a gush of amniotic fluid.

This can't be right, I thought. There are still three weeks to go until my due date.

I hoisted myself up from the couch to George's moans of displeasure and waddled into the bathroom to see what was going on. On the way, more amniotic fluid ran down my legs. I yelled up to Craig to come downstairs so I could apprise him of the situation.

---

1. Think big, blow-up, insulated rubber wading pool that has a heating system and water-jet action.

Craig called Leah, whom we'd chosen to be our midwife. We'd interviewed several midwives, but from the moment Leah walked into our house, we knew she was the one. Calm, centered, and gentle, she also exuded strength, wisdom, and experience. I loved her immediately and knew we would be in good hands.

Except, when Leah arrived at our house later that evening, just as my contractions were really starting to pick up, she explained that the birthing tub we'd ordered was still at the home of the woman who was expecting her baby before me. So here we were, contractions every six minutes or so apart, sans tub.

Not to worry. Leah had borrowed a large Rubbermaid tub from a friend, which we could fill with warm water so that I could still have a water-birth. Upon inspecting the tub, George remarked that it looked strikingly similar to the kind of feed basin he had seen cattle eating and drinking from at Wolfe's Neck Farm, which we'd recently visited.

"That's exactly what it is," Leah said. "It does the job, though. Let's get started filling it up."

The next morning, on my hands and knees in the cattle trough of warm water, with Craig[2] right by my side with cool washcloths and barf bags, I hit that place between Scylla and Charybdis, and pleaded with Leah to make it stop.

"I can't do this!" I barked.

And Leah said, "Yes, you can. You are right where you need to be. You're ready to have that baby.

2. George was being held at bay by Chuck, Craig's father, somewhere downstairs.

"Listen," Leah continued, "there's a deep connection between your mouth and your cervix. Right now, you are clamping your mouth shut. I want you to open your mouth up as wide as you can. When you're comfortable with yourself, you can open up and say what you need to say and do what you need to do and let your voice come out. Open your mouth up as wide as you can and move through the pain and the hard work. Find your strength and open up completely. The wider you open your mouth, the wider your cervix will open up. And then your baby will come out into the world."

And so I opened my mouth as wide as I could and screamed bloody murder. Soon, my body did that violent and guttural uterine-wrenching thing, and—an eternity or so later—our baby slid out of my body and into the warm water. Leah scooped her up and handed her to me. I held her little being close and it was perfect and beautiful and glowy.

After Craig bravely snipped the umbilical cord, the placenta came out—and that was not so beautiful. It was absolutely hideous and looked like something out of *Alien*. Leah put the placenta into a bowl and took it over to the window to examine it.

And we were there, Craig and I, with our baby girl, whom we named Dora, which means gift. George ran upstairs to join us soon afterward and jumped up on the bed to meet his sister, and now we were a family of four.

The LabΘrinth

"One is harassed, both day and night, by the divine being
that is the image of the living self within the locked labyrinth
of one's own disoriented psyche. . . . Here, instead of passing
outward, beyond the confines of the visible world,
the hero goes inward, to be born again."

10 CENTIMETERS

ora's arrival really got the Hausfrau
adventure rolling. There was something about having
two: the yin and the yang, the push and the pull, the
agony and the ecstasy. This became especially evident
at nighttime, while the rest of the Western hemisphere
slept.

Like her brother before her, Dora nursed every two
hours, day and night (and would continue to do so well
into her second year of life). She slept in our bed, as did
George, who could not tolerate being alone. I lay there
one night, in the middle of our queen-size bed, sand-
wiched between my babes, Craig snoring away on the
other side of George. I was the queen of our bed: a
queen awash in a sea composed of breast milk and hormones—but, alas, not serotonin.

Complex emotions swept over me like a wave: I was
at once grateful for my family and this moment, yet I
felt as though I was suffocating. My body was exhausted yet electric. I had to get out of that bed. And I
needed to write. For the first time in six years, I felt the
call of the muse.

The call was coming directly from the journal that
Grammy Mil had given me so many years before.
When we'd moved to Maine, I'd packed it away in a
box that contained old photo albums from our B.C.
days and some of my writing samples and short stories.

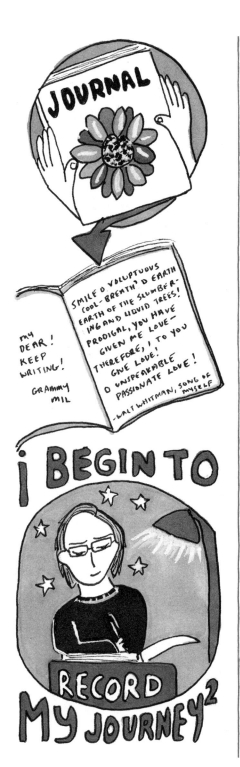

I extracted myself from my family's legs and arms and went downstairs, to rummage through that box marked "memorabilia" in the front entryway. I knew it was there: my journal, with the bright sunflower on the cover that Milly had painted in golden oils.

Reunited with my grandmother's gift, I felt the surge of the muse. I clicked on the living-room light and sat on the couch. With black marker in hand, I began to write about my days.

Journal entry one—[date? 3:30 a.m.]

I am lost in the LabOrinth[1]—a maze of hormones, identity issues, exhaustion, ego struggles, and physical depletion. I am restless and overwhelmed with contradictory emotions. I love the kids so much, but I feel like there's nothing left of *me*. I'm mired in the overwhelming day-to-day responsibilities of taking care of a newborn and a "spirited" four-year-old as well as struggling to come to grips with the mind-blowing changes that having a baby can bring about.

1. In preparation for Dora's birth, I read a book called *Birthing from Within*, in which the author, Pam England, herself a midwife and a mother, coins the term "LabOrinth" and goes on to write: "The labyrinth is a sacred symbol of Life. It represents the roller coaster drama in our lives, our neurotic decision-making process, and the body itself. Our brains, intestines, and circulatory system, and even the first journey we make from our father to our mother, and from the center of our mother's body into the world, are labyrinthine. The labyrinth is also a sacred symbol of labor. A woman's psychic and physical journey from maidenhood-to-motherhood during labor, and again postpartum, is surely a labyrinth." Ms. England has posited that it takes a woman three years postpartum to emerge from the LabOrinth.

2. The words "journey" and "journal" come from the same root: the Latin word *diurnum,* meaning "of the day."

I remember that right after I gave birth to George, Mom and Dad were visiting, and Dad offered a little nugget of parenting encouragement (see Fig. 1). Looking back at it now, I think it was his way of saying that the loss of identity I was experiencing was just the beginning of the journey, and that it would behoove me to get comfy with that idea ASAP. But I thought for sure he was wrong. Certainly with time this parenting gig would get easier—once the babes started "sleeping through the night" (a phenomenon I have yet to witness) and/or were out of diapers and/or started eating solid foods and/or went to school.

But Dad's right. Even though I've had almost half a decade to hone my mothering skills, there is this incredibly profound intensity with which I feel everything now. It's as if having babies stripped away some sort of protective outer layer (sanity?) and now the world and all of its stimuli—in all of its beauty and hideousness—penetrate me like sand inside an oyster shell. Each day that goes by, my life feels more and more full, so full, in fact, that some days I'll surely burst.

This afternoon, when Dora fell asleep nursing, I called Lynne to chat for a while, and she told me about the time her mother-in-law said the following about a friend who was putting her energy into raising her children: "She was an intellectual and a really gifted writer, but now she's just a hausfrau."

Oof!

What was that about? Was the comment a personal dis to Lynne, who herself is a gifted writer and teacher but spends most of her time catering to the needs of two children under four? Or was it a manifestation of the mother-in-law's own fear of insignificance in her struggle for identity? Or was it a shrewd reflection of the way we belittle mothers in our society, no matter which path we choose? It doesn't matter, because whatever the answer is—and I suspect it's a combination of all of the above—it just plain sucks. It sucks because it implies that by making the sacrifices demanded of motherhood, the friend simultaneously lost her intellect and her gift for writing. What a brazen, insulting leap in logic! It doesn't make any sense! And yet, we walk around with this sentiment nestled snugly in our consciousness.

Surely, Lynne's mother-in-law must have herself experienced the daily roller coaster of passion (complete adoration of your offspring one instant, abject hatred the next), the exhausting drudgery (here, let's put that snow boot on again, little one, so we can then struggle into your hat, mittens, and coat and then get your baby sister ready in the same fashion so that we can then trudge out to the car and nearly kill ourselves on the ice in the driveway while I wrestle you into your car seats and then drive to the grocery store, where I will attempt to make mindful food choices for my family while you pull items off the shelves and scream for point-of-purchase candy), and the conundrums (should I let my infant chew on that crayon for a moment—it does say non-toxic on the box, after all—so that I can attend to my four-year-old's hysteria for having gotten a poop smear on his Red Power Ranger costume?).

My question is: How could Lynne's mother-in-law have said such a thing? Thought such a thing of a fellow hausfrau? How could she forget that every single minute of a hausfrau's day is a tangled web of intense thought and emotion? How could she belittle someone else's experience as less important or meaningful or deep than her own?

I think it's because there is a hausfrau amnesia—some magical mind eraser that blots out the struggles we experience on a daily basis.

I believe it's the only way we can get out of bed in the morning and do it all over again. It's also why our species survives. But those struggles are precisely what we need to keep in mind, because our voices are lost when we don't tell the stories that make up our days.

I've decided that I'm going to record that roller coaster ride I'm on every day. It's not going to last forever, I know it, but this is the way my life is right now. And this is the way I'm trying to cope. I *am* a hausfrau, dammit!

Or rather, I am *the* Hausfrau!

3. Contents of behemoth tote bag: two sunscreens (SPF 45 for the kids; SPF 4 for my sun-worshipping self); five condoms (a year's supply, folks!); two plastic sand shovels; smushed Newman's Own Fig Newmans in a resealable baggie; *The New Yorker;* an apple-juice box; a sippy cup with rancid liquid inside; three diapers; fruit-juice-sweetened lollipops for use as bribery; a rancid cheese-stick nubbin; an apple with pen marks on it; wipes; my journal; black pens; wallet; keys; cell phone.

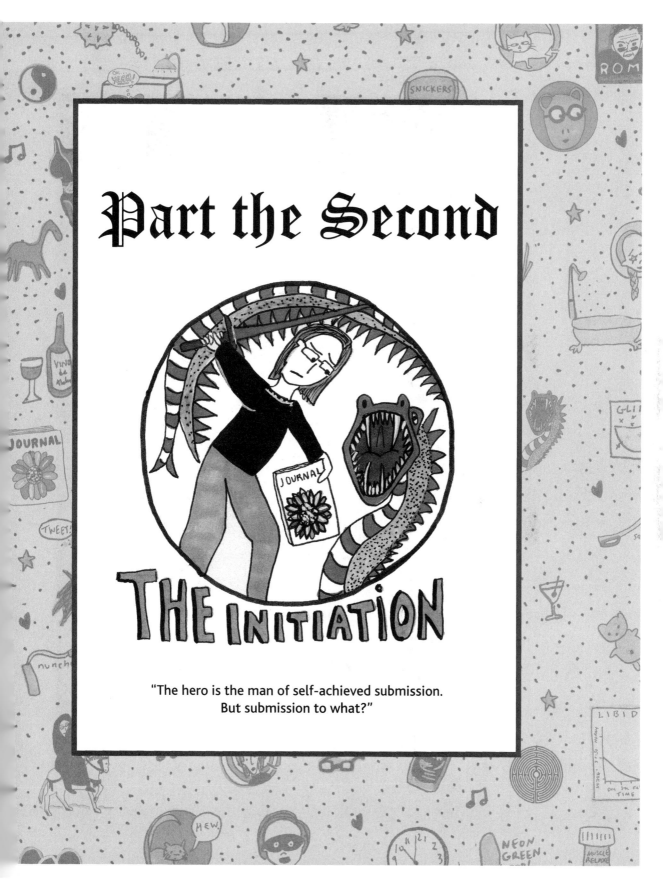

Part the Second

THE INITIATION

"The hero is the man of self-achieved submission.
But submission to what?"

The Road of Trials
The Fourteen Labors of the Hausfrau

"Once having traversed the threshold, the hero moves in a dream landscape of curiously fluid, ambiguous forms, where he must survive a succession of trials. This is a favorite phase of the myth-adventure. It has produced a world literature of miraculous tests and ordeals."

10 CENTIMETERS!

One: Home Renovation, or How It Came to Be that I Sat in Cat Diarrhea

round about the start of the new millennium, Craig and I began to renovate our ramshackle Victorian. We were in a serious state of denial (you could even say we were delusional), sharing dreams à la *It's a Wonderful Life* that we would fix up the severely neglected old place, fill it with light and color, and turn it into a home of our very own making. When we did the walk-through with our realtor for the first time, I didn't notice the details that would later drive me to the brink of insanity (e.g., falling-apart front steps, a paved backyard with a collapsing shed, faux wood linoleum paneling and dropped ceilings that covered a multitude of sins, a bathroom floor made of some crumbling green substance that stuck to our bare feet, etc., etc.), so caught up was I in the house's potential.

We bought the house for a song. It had belonged to a tired city employee, who apparently had a penchant for Disney keepsakes, bacon, and contact paper as a decorating medium. She also had never thought to clean the place and had needed to get the hell out of Dodge ASAP.

On moving day, the guys we hired abandoned our piano on the sidewalk in front of the house after attempting to hoist it through the narrow, winding front entryway for several hours. Was this an omen?

Inside, the house reeked of bacon and had a measurable amount of grease covering every surface—including the keyholes. When I turned on the overhead light in the room that was to be George's, there was a loud pop, a sizzle, the lights went out, and then the house started to fill up with smoke. We called the fire department and an electrician, who needed to completely dismantle the Byzantine crisscross of wires and charged us $800 to do so. A week later, part of the ceiling in that same room collapsed and landed on the pillow on George's bed. Thank goodness our son was co-sleeping in our bed—with *us*.

It was a fucked-up mess, but it was *our* fucked-up mess. And we were determined to transform it, one room at a time, staying always mindful of our shared vision. The plan was this: Craig would remain unemployed so that he could work on converting the third floor (i.e., the unfinished attic) into three bedrooms and a bathroom while starting up a nonprofit organization called Cultivating Community. We would live on the second floor and rent the first floor out to cover the mortgage. Our tenants: a single mom named Taurus, her six-year-old daughter, Tammy, and her eighteen-month-old son, Reggie. Once Craig's nonprofit became stable, we would proceed with the second-floor renovations, such as knocking down walls, building other walls, putting in a new kitchen and bathrooms, and dealing with the lead paint abatement. Finally, we would completely overhaul the exterior of the house, as it presently consisted of rotten wood held together with flaking lead paint.

Good plan! Problem was, we possessed none of the tools necessary for a decade-long foray into complete home renovation: reliable childcare, yogi-like self-discipline, patience, and money. Some days I was ready to sell the squalid construction site to the first bidder, get rid of all of our crap, and move to Mexico. But then there was the promise of renewal, and that had me hooked.

We entrusted the tearing-down and building-back of walls to a contractor named Kenny, who was charged with creating the spaces that would become our kitchen, bathroom, and family room. Kenny found it necessary to leave a heaping pile of debris in the middle of our home, which he apparently didn't think was part of his job to clean up.

Dora had just learned to crawl and—similar to the way our geriatric cross-eyed cat, Shlomo, would automatically jump on my freshly laundered black shirt no matter where I'd placed it in the room—she was drawn to the gargantuan pile of caustic refuse.

In addition, George (who was then four and a half) couldn't wait to get his hands on the sharp wooden sticks jutting out from the pile. He pretended they were swords and brandished them enthusiastically.

I became an absolute nervous wreck and spent most of my energy devising schemes to keep the kids out of the house. I was also hoping to avoid the parade of workmen, who appeared in our living quarters at all hours and who arrived with zero notice.

Kenny worked hard but was a tad absentminded. For example, we went away for a few days that summer, during the initial tear-down portion of the renovation. Kenny unplugged our fridge, forgetting, I guess, that there must be food inside. Before we had left, I had purchased hundreds of dollars worth of frozen foods (pizzas, chickens, juices) that we could eat with minimal preparation. These items, along with everything else in the fridge, sat festering during a heat wave. Upon our return, Craig had the honor of donning protective gear and cleaning up the godforsaken mess.

Kenny had also neglected to tape plastic to the doorways, to prevent plaster dust from the walls he tore down from spreading throughout the house. Oops! The result? A measurable amount of plaster dust covering every surface of our home. And instead of remedying the situation before we returned home, Kenny left the mess for us to deal with! Thanks, Kenny!

So I tried my hardest to create healthy play options for the kids—*outside* of the house. One diversion involved ordering George a Spider-Man costume from Suitsme, a vintage clothing and costume rental shop that has since gone out of business. The woman who owned the shop said it would take a week for it to arrive. Suffice it to say that that week crept along at an excruciatingly slow pace for all involved.

On Friday, we drove over to Suitsme, but the owner had been out of the shop—getting rolfed, no less—during delivery hours, so the Spider-Man costume was in postal limbo. The scene George created in the shop made me consider arranging for an exorcism.

Come Monday, we visited Suitsme yet again and, this time, finally left with the costume. We then got ready to go over to Shaw's grocery store to protest genetically engineered food—a project I had been roped into when a woman from Greenpeace emailed me and suggested I represent hausfraus everywhere who care about what our children are eating. I prepared by memorizing tracts of information she sent me on genetically engineered food so that I would appear knowledgeable and articulate when approached by the media.

We dressed in eye-catching yet casual apparel and stood in the Shaw's parking lot with the Greenpeace contingent for two sweltering hours until we were shooed off the property by the store manager, who threatened police intervention. Nary a media person approached us.

The following morning, I awoke with a fever (unbeknownst to me, I had developed walking pneumonia) and also discovered that Kenny had turned off all the water in our house so he could frig with something in our kitchen-to-be. The temperature outside was a blazing 92 degrees by 10:00 a.m. And so, with greasy, feverish face, I packed up our stuff and sought the oasis of the wading pool and fountains at Deering Oaks Park.

We'd left the house in a hurry, and I didn't notice that our unfortunate cat, Shlomo, asleep on our bed, got shut in the bedroom when a hot wind blew the door closed.

We spent the day at the park—the kids frolicking in the fountain, me sweating bullets from my fever. The media—who had completely ignored us during the Shaw's action—now swarmed around us. For some unexplainable reason, they had decided to come to Deering Oaks that day to interview moms about a rash of child abductions in California.

In my feverish haze, I could barely construct a sentence. Luckily, they mixed up the moms' names when the segment aired on the news that night.

When we got home that evening, I herded the kids right upstairs—circumventing the pile o' debris—to get them ready for bed in time for me to catch myself (appearing as Emily Smith of Freeport) on the six o'clock news. I opened the bedroom door (Shlomo looked at me sheepishly, I realized in retrospect, and then hightailed it outta there) and I went over to sit down on the bed to change Dora's diaper.

I sat. Oddly, my brain didn't register the sound or the feeling but rather, the putrefying smell. As I continued to diaper my writhing infant, I thought, "That's funny, she smells like a nasty poop—but she's totally clean." It was at that moment that I looked down to discover the horror that I was seated upon.

This all happened years ago. Our house is still in process and Shlomo is no longer with us (see page 188 for details). But his memory lives on! And so does the stain on my favorite white comforter. And just think: If the cat feces had been firm, well-contained, and discreetly deposited, I wouldn't have had an ending for this story.

Two: Monsterfrau! or Hell Hath No Fury Like a Hausfrau with No Serotonin

HEAD FULL O' SNOOZING VIPERS HELD AT BAY BY 32 SEROTONIN MOLECULES

MONSTERFRAU

(LATENT PHASE)

SERENELY CRAFTING DRIED LEAF ARRANGEMENTS WITH KINDER

he brain of an adult female needs four hours of uninterrupted sleep each night in order to produce serotonin. And just in case you've let your subscription to *The New England Journal of Medicine* lapse, serotonin is one of the chemicals responsible for an individual's ability to cope with stress. It also produces a sense of well-being.

By my calculations, and given my children's sleep cycles—or, to be more precise, their night-waking cycles—by the time Dora was two, my brain hadn't been able to produce serotonin for roughly six years. Just as soon as George started "sleeping through the night," at age four, Dora was born. She nursed through the wee hours with the gusto of a newborn well into her second year.

I have to face facts. The lack of forty winks over the years has rendered me the hausfrau equivalent of Dr. Jekyll and Mr. Hyde. I can be joyful, relaxed, and level-headed—making pancakes with the kids, frolicking in the snow, dancing in the living room, lovingly wiping butts and noses, feeding the cat with generosity, feeling that my home is welcoming, organized, and pleasing, etc. This state of being usually lasts for two or three hours after breakfast. At these times, I look at the world and at my life and think, *All is as it should be. Yes. This is good!*

But then. As the thirty-two molecules of serotonin that my brain has miraculously manufactured the night before begin to dwindle, and as the day progresses and

the inevitable stresses pile up . . . look out! Some time around 5:20 p.m., a creature emerges—so heinous and vile that she can only be called by one name: **MONSTERFRAU!**

And this is how it all unfolds:

A slapping match ensues between Dora and George while I'm on the phone trying to make an appointment to have their blood lead levels tested.[1] Because the agency I'm dealing with is DHS (the Department of Human Services), I calmly and creatively refocus my kids by promising to make smoothies after I'm off the phone.

While making smoothies, Dora grabs the yogurt container, turns it upside down, and lets go. The full quart drops to the floor.

As I'm cleaning up the yogurt, Dora strips down naked and pees on the living-room rug. She had been chanting the word "pee-pee" over and over again moments before, and like an idiot, I'd ignored her.

While I'm cleaning up the urine, Dora poops in her little potty and then tries to dump her feces into the big toilet, dropping a big runny chunk of said feces on the bathroom rug.

---

1. During our home renovation, Kenny had knocked down several walls in the kitchen, releasing toxic lead-paint dust into the air. Although the dust and paint and hellish mess were thoroughly "abated" by the contractor DHS hired to help us, I still obsessively test my children's blood-lead levels, as even a trace of the stuff can cause learning disabilities, ADHD, and liver damage.

Dora runs out of the bathroom, yelling "Poop! Poop!" and commences wrestling with George, who screams in response.

Lunchtime. Since the yogurt for our smoothies went bye-bye, I search our refrigerator for some protein-based foodstuff for the kids to eat. They beg for Annie's Mac & Cheese, but we are out of milk and butter—as well as yogurt.[2]

I decide to make miso soup. George announces that he hates tofu. Dora mimics him.

Time to do errands! I drive to Rainbow Toys to buy a present for George's friend who's turning six this upcoming weekend. Dora decides to sit on a contraption that resembles a pogo stick, collapsing both it and a display of rubber balls.

George decides that his friend must have an "I Dig Ancient Egypt!" excavation kit for his birthday, which includes a pyramid made of sand, in which are lodged several "artifacts" that the child is meant to dig out with sharp metal tools. I hesitate, thinking of the sand flying all over the room, then decide that the mother probably already thinks I'm a freak anyway, so what the hell!

George begs for an "I Dig Ancient Egypt!" kit for himself. I cave and purchase a second box of $30 sand.

---

2. My children like their Annie's Mac & Cheese prepared two different ways, as follows. George enjoys his mixed only with plain yogurt, as it creates a richer sauce with more tang and mouthfeel. Dora prefers hers mixed with milk and butter, like it calls for in the directions.

Dora howls from exhaustion and hunger and lies down on the floor in front of the cash register.

Back in the car, George repeatedly asks if we can listen to the radio. He commands me to turn the dial to 94.3, home to WCYY—Portland's Rock Alternative! I worry that the lyrics in the Green Day song "American Idiot"[3] are inappropriate for my six- and two-year-olds, even though I agree with the band's message. I turn the volume down. George complains that he can't hear. When I turn up the volume, Dora yells that it's too loud. They argue in this fashion for several minutes.

George announces that he's hungry. Dora reminds me that she's hungry, too. I have forgotten snacks[4] yet again.

I decide to go grocery shopping and am thrown into my usual quandary about which store I should patronize: the wildly expensive but locally owned Whole Grocer or the wildly expensive national franchise Wild Oats,[5] which beckons with its deli that carries chicken wings, Dora's favorite.

I pull into Wild Oats, able to brush aside my pangs of guilt because George has jumped out of the car before I've pulled to a stop in the parking space. He rushes into the path of an oncoming SUV.

---

3. The lyrics: "Don't want to be an American idiot. . . . /And can you hear the sound of hysteria?/The subliminal mind-fuck, America."

4. When in God's name will I learn to pack snacks?

5. Both have since been bought by the even larger wildly expensive Whole Foods Market.

Safely inside Wild Oats, we journey to the deli, where we learn that they are out of chicken wings. Dora does not understand this. She shouts at me and will accept no substitutes.

Frantically, I throw items into the grocery cart, which, in combination with what I have in my cupboards at home,[6] might make an evening meal. My attention to detail is compromised, however, by George, who—in the throes of imaginative play—hangs off the cart with one hand and sings sea chanteys.

I head over to the checkout, where my debit card is declined because, in my serotonin-deprived haze, I can't remember my PIN, even though I've had the same card and PIN for the past five and a half years. I fruitlessly punch in numbers—but in which order do they go? The three customers behind me shuffle their feet and sigh and clear their throats. I want to drop to the floor at the cash register and shout, "I am a fragile and vulnerable human being! Please take pity on me!" But I don't have to, because the cashier lets me write a check, God bless her.

I'm convinced I have early-onset Alzheimer's.

Dora falls asleep in the car on the way home, and since she's "nontransferable"—meaning that she wakes up the moment I try to pick her up—I let her snooze in her car seat, which I lug up two flights of stairs before unpacking the groceries and putting them away, checking my e-mail, and returning phone calls.

Our tenant drops by and announces that her daughter has lice.

---

6. A bag of stale cranberries, a can of tomato sauce, a very old box of falafel mix, and a bag of some grain that I bought in bulk a year ago when I was trying to introduce more whole foods into our diet but have no idea how to cook or even identify. It looks like couscous, but it is not, I assure you.

I grab George and check his scalp, while he wriggles and shouts at me and twists his head back and forth. I don't see anything of concern . . . yet.

"Quiet time" for George. I send him to his room to "rest" so that I can have a few moments to myself.

I sit on the couch near Dora, hoping to steal a chunk of time to write in my journal. The moment I place my pen to paper, Dora's eyelids flutter open.

While I nurse Dora on the couch, the phone rings. My instinct tells me to ignore it, but I pick up. It's my mother, wondering whether we would like fingertip towels for Christmas. Since she's already purchased them, I don't have the heart to tell her no—and that all the towels she's given us for the last ten Christmases are lying in a gargantuan terry-cloth heap in our attic—so I put the phone down and manage several deep breaths.

George jumps on the couch next to me, upsetting Dora and announcing that he wants to dress up as a royal knight. I am to be his squire.

I hang up with my mother, and when Dora's finished draining my milk supply, I attend to George, who demands that I pin on his cape. Since I can't find any safety pins in the house, I inventively use a clothespin to secure the cape, and milord runs outside to play with Tammy.

High-pitched screams issue from the backyard. I haul ass downstairs with Dora on my hip to discover that George has punctured Tammy's chin—by accident—while sword-fighting.

I drag a hollering George back upstairs to reinforce the consequences of rough weapon play. I notice that he is now wearing the cap that moments before was on Tammy's (lice-ridden) head.

I allow George to watch PBS while I make dinner. *Liberty's Kids*[7] is on. He asks me why the Revolutionary War was OK but the Iraq War is not. I rack my muddled brain for an answer and tell him I'll explain later.

7. Thank God for PBS Kids programming! I can relax knowing that he is *learning* something (in this case, about the Battle of Bunker Hill in the Revolutionary War) while hypnotized by the screen.

Zoom comes on the tube, and it's a devil's bargain. George does this thing whenever he watches *Zoom*: If the *Zoom* kids are making a snack or a craft, George yells for me to come over and watch so I'll learn how to execute the snack/craft, with the idea that we can make it together later.

If I ignore him and keep cooking, George yells louder. If I come over to watch the *Zoom* kids, I have to leave my garlic sizzling away on the stove. Hausfrau dilemma! Should I turn off the TV and discipline him for yelling? That doesn't feel right, because, after all, he's just excited about making watermelon smoothies together—like the *Zoom* kids. Ah, jeez.

Craig steps through the door, refreshed and bright-eyed after attending a conference all day for nonprofit directors. He informs me that one of the workshops he sat in on had to do with organizing space and reducing clutter. After eight hours of sitting on his butt listening to some woman who gets paid big bucks to tell others how to organize their environments, he has oodles of groovy vibes and positive energy to share with Dora, as she runs naked through the kitchen, wielding paint-brushes.

Craig suggests that we consider hiring the consultant who ran the workshop to come help us organize our cluttered, chaotic, and befuddled lives.

Whoops! Not a good choice, Daddy! Look out! It's . . . MONSTERFRAU!

I beat a hasty retreat into our bedroom, where I cry uncontrollably for twenty minutes and then emerge, feeling fresh and calm and clear-headed.[8]

I finish making the family's evening meal, which is nourishing but overly seasoned with burned garlic.

---

8. I have since postulated that crying really hard generates more serotonin than just about anything. Except four hours of uninterrupted sleep.

Three: Pestilence!

ince becoming parents, Craig and I have encountered all manner of childhood afflictions. Every year since George was a newborn, we've dealt with some sort of health issue that may have been seriously trying at the time but from which we learned and emerged relatively unscathed.

But then, we hadn't yet dealt with lice.

Lice: the parasite so irritating and tenacious that we entered a new level of day-to-day coping—based entirely upon the eradication of this species from our heads and living quarters.

The lice picked a really bad time to set up shop on our scalps. We'd just received word that we had ten days to pack up all our stuff and move out of our house for six weeks so that city-contracted workmen could remove the lead paint inside our home. Eerily, the lice decided to move *in* that same day.

We'll pause from our story for a moment for Lice 101, supplied by the Bayer Corporation, makers of outrageously priced lice-removal shampoos, gels, combs, and sprays. Through their brochure and others like it, we learned so much about our tiny visitors! For example: Lice can hold their breath for long periods of time, which is why attempting to drown them in the bathtub is an exercise in futility. I tried anyway—several times.

Even though head lice are extremely common—most everyone I confided in during our infestation had a yarn to spin about them—I was absolutely horrified.

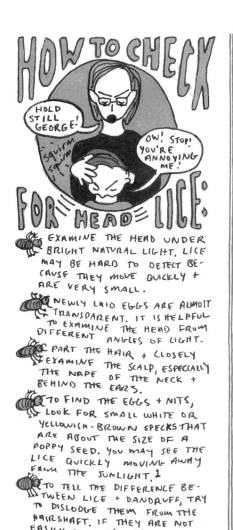

HOW TO CHECK FOR HEAD LICE

HOLD STILL GEORGE!

—squirm squirm—

OW! STOP! YOU'RE ANNOYING ME!

- EXAMINE THE HEAD UNDER BRIGHT NATURAL LIGHT. LICE MAY BE HARD TO DETECT BECAUSE THEY MOVE QUICKLY + ARE VERY SMALL.
- NEWLY LAID EGGS ARE ALMOST TRANSPARENT. IT IS HELPFUL TO EXAMINE THE HEAD FROM DIFFERENT ANGLES OF LIGHT.
- PART THE HAIR + CLOSELY EXAMINE THE SCALP, ESPECIALLY THE NAPE OF THE NECK + BEHIND THE EARS.
- TO FIND THE EGGS + NITS, LOOK FOR SMALL WHITE OR YELLOWISH-BROWN SPECKS THAT ARE ABOUT THE SIZE OF A POPPY SEED. YOU MAY SEE THE LICE QUICKLY MOVING AWAY FROM THE SUNLIGHT.[1]
- TO TELL THE DIFFERENCE BETWEEN LICE + DANDRUFF, TRY TO DISLODGE THEM FROM THE HAIRSHAFT. IF THEY ARE NOT EASILY REMOVED, THEY ARE PROBABLY EGGS.

TOOLS OF THE TRADE

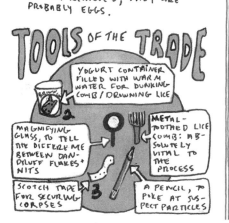

YOGURT CONTAINER FILLED WITH WARM WATER FOR DUNKING COMB/DROWNING LICE

MAGNIFYING GLASS, TO TELL THE DIFFERENCE BETWEEN DANDRUFF FLAKES + NITS

METAL-TOOTHED LICE COMB: ABSOLUTELY VITAL TO THE PROCESS

SCOTCH TAPE FOR SECURING CORPSES

A PENCIL, TO POKE AT SUSPECT PARTICLES

I think it was the whole "parasite" aspect: It's just plain disgusting to be a "host" to a blood-sucking, microscopic insect that lays its eggs in your frigging hair.

The next ten days were a blur of laundry (sheets, pillowcases, blankets, and clothes had to be washed daily in hot water to kill any of the lice unfortunate enough to have wandered off our noggins), packing (I had sworn that I was going to be methodical and organized but ended up throwing our belongings willy-nilly into battered, bursting boxes), and pesticide applications. I really didn't want to move into our temporary digs with infested heads and, between bouts of freaking out completely, I did manage to secure George's scalp as a lice-free zone. I chose to use an herbal remedy on him, and it worked. (See my recipe at the bottom of the facing page.)

The combing is the key to lice eradication, because if even one egg is left, you're guaranteed a pate full of lice within a week to ten days. This fact forcefully encouraged OCD-like combing, checking, and rechecking of my kids' heads by this here hausfrau!

Luckily, and perhaps because she's free of so much worldly taint, Dora never got the parasites at all. I liberally doused her little head with tea tree oil to prevent infestation. And I was able to prevent reinfestation with George in the same manner.

---

1. Is that not just so positively grotesque and vampiric?

2. Courtesy of Lynne Rowe.

3. Courtesy of Ayun Halliday.

Here's some more info about lice:

"Head lice are tiny, wingless insects that live on the human scalp (clean heads, usually). They are about as big as sesame seeds. Head lice sustain themselves by sucking blood—just as mosquitoes do. However, unlike mosquitoes, lice cannot fly or jump from one person to another; they can only crawl. Children often get head lice from head-to-head contact with other children, but may also get them by sharing personal items such as hats, combs, or headbands.[4]

"Eggs are laid by the female louse. They are about the size of a poppy seed and are difficult to see because their color easily blends in with the infested [person's] hair. Eggs are laid near the root of the hair and are attached with a waterproof, glue-like substance that can't be washed or blown away.

"Nits are the empty eggshells left behind when lice hatch from eggs. Dandruff, sand, and flakes of hairspray are commonly mistaken for eggs or nits. Eggs and nits are not easily removed and must be carefully combed out with a fine-toothed comb.

"Nits vary in color—from yellowish-brown to white. Since the hair grows, nits are usually found further away from the root of the hair. Many schools have a 'No Nit Policy,' which means children who have had head lice are not readmitted to school until all the nits are gone. If your child has head lice, it is very important to comb out eggs and nits as part of the lice elimination process."[5]

4. Or jaunty squire's caps belonging to our tenant's daughter.

5. This information, as well as the tips in "How to Check for Head Lice" on page 70, is taken from "All About Lice," courtesy of Bayer HealthCare (www.ridlice.com).

Though Craig and I faithfully treated ourselves with every lice-killing product on the market and checked each other with the frequency of a pair of female gorillas, our heads full o' lice refused to give up their little lice ghosts. Our tenant, Taurus, said it was because lice love thick, coarse hair, which we both have, but I'm convinced we brought the scourge upon ourselves with an act of premeditated bad karma so outrageous that I feared we'd be infested for the rest of our known days.

Halloween arrived, and we carved pumpkins and got all dressed up and went trick-or-treating: a Viking, a pumpkin, and two lice-infested maniacs. We came home and got jacked up on candy amid the stacks of boxes in our disassembled home.

The next day we moved into our temporary shelter: a hotel in downtown Portland. The lice came with us.

As is true in any family, we all dealt with our stress with varying coping tools. I started drinking red wine from the Rhone Valley. Craig suffered from insomnia and spent the wee hours writing grants for his nonprofit organization on his laptop, meanwhile secretly pillaging the kids' Halloween candy. I caught him one night and joined in. Amazingly, we spawned a child (George) who prefers candy of the sour ilk (e.g., Smarties, Swee-TARTS), so we had a plethora of chocolates on which to gorge ourselves.

Dora took comfort at my breast and nursed at night again with the gusto of a newborn, while George thrived in our new environs and spent many hours jumping off the top bunk in his spacious digs. He took to wearing his Viking warrior costume at all times and decided he wanted to be called "Ron."

Because those who knew of our plight didn't want to come anywhere near our lice-infested selves, and since we feared infesting others, we basically just hunkered down for six weeks. We started to go a little nutty in our exile by week two, so I arranged for a brave babysitter to come and watch the kids so Craig and I could get out for a big night on the town. We ate Chinese food and then went to the Nickelodeon to see *Mystic River*,[6] starring Sean Penn. Throughout the movie I kept feeling like I had lice running around on my head. I couldn't wait to get home to do a treatment.

This time, I chose a more radical approach: Craig shaved my head with an electric razor in the kitchen of our temporary shelter, and then we treated ourselves with pesticides and spent the remainder of that romantic eve combing nits out of each other's hair.

6. Review of *Mystic River*: Holy shit! This movie was about as uplifting as a head full o' lice! I love Sean Penn, as you know, and would pay a hefty sum just to watch the guy sit in a La-Z-Boy for two hours, so it did me good to see him on the screen. But I found the movie itself—chock full of brutal murders, child molestation, and wifely betrayal—to be gratuitously gut-wrenching and the writing heavy-handed. I guess I'm just a little tired of movies about men who kill each other.

In a strange way, I grew to enjoy our exile. It was a vacation from our lead-contaminated home, where Craig and I had spent every waking moment (that we weren't directly engaged in parenting, working, or preparing/eating a meal) trying to fix the place up. I let go of my inner neat-freak and settled into a refreshing bout of slovenliness. We got a lot of takeout (justified by the lack of cupboards or counter space in the temporary kitchen), read Harry Potter books aloud, and went for long walks downtown. Dora painted many pictures, which we taped up to decorate the barren gray walls. I read Eckhart Tolle's *The Power of Now* and worked really hard on staying in the moment.

I commiserated on the phone with my sister Boo in Seattle, who had gotten lice in India a few years back. We analyzed the situation by deconstructing the social and cultural implications of lice eradication, and she and I grew closer through our shared experience.

Lice infestation also prompted me to become intimately familiar with the floor plans of CVS, where I shopped for pesticides, and Wild Oats, where I bought tea tree oil because it was on sale. The clerks at these establishments took pity on me and welcomed me into the fold of the lice-ridden.

I met many dear fellow hausfraus while haunting the aisles of CVS (which—ironically?—stands for "convenience, value, and service"). They all had stories to weave and tips to share.

One frau's eyes welled up with tears as she described her experience the previous year trying to comb the parasites out of her daughter's waist-length hair. She implored me to seal up our bare pillows in garbage bags and then put the cases on, trapping and suffocating the lice within. She also told me to put all the kids' stuffed animals in large trash bags and store them away for six weeks. She said I'd also better start vacuuming the carpeted floors in our temporary digs a couple of times a day and should definitely spray the couches with pesticides in aerosol form. She squeezed my arm and whispered, "Good luck," as I trudged out of CVS with new resolve, armed with a Thanksgiving bounty of lice-killing products.

And speaking of the products, there are many and they're expensive. We tried them all, and I can tell you this: The most effective remedy is to shave your head. Barring that, you can use the tea tree oil recipe on page 71 and then enlist a loved one to patiently comb the nits out, hour after hour, day after day, week after week. Use tea tree oil shampoo and conditioner to prevent reinfestation.

I've since heard that good old-fashioned mayonnaise, spread liberally on the hair for a few hours under a plastic shower cap, works well, and you can buy a quart of mayo for what you'd spend on an ounce of Rid. I've also since learned that Cetaphil, the body lotion you can buy over-the-counter at any drug store, works better than the pesticides.[7]

Yes, the shaving worked and we managed to successfully remove the pests from our heads just in time to move back into our newly lead-free home, which was also freshly painted and sparkling clean—right before the Christmas holidays. Our heads were irritated from all the products we'd been dumping on ourselves, which left us with severe itchiness: the very same symptom that the lice had caused. Of course, this led to hours of checking and rechecking—and to confusing dry, flaking scalp for nits, which thus caused many post-infestation freak-outs. But, in the end, the lice were gone, the lead was gone, and we were *home*.

---

7. Tip courtesy of Anna, Charlie, and Emma, who dealt with the scourge three times when they lived in Puerto Rico.

Four: How It Came to Be that I Tried to Squeeze My Enormous Ass into Brazilian Surfing Shorts

n our eleventh anniversary, Craig and I decided to celebrate in style. We'd gotten married back in 1993 in Provincetown, Massachusetts, and we thought it would be fun to revisit the scene. My folks generously offered to watch the kids for the weekend, which was convenient, since they live on Cape Cod, an hour's drive from Provincetown.

So on a Friday evening in June, we put the kids in their pajamas, packed up, and departed after a nourishing dinner—Craig and I toting huge travel mugs full of coffee. Our strategy was to stay alert after the kids fell asleep so that we could have a conversation. Life had gotten away from us, it seemed, and it had been weeks since we had shared more than a few conciliatory grunts.

Perhaps it was the caffeine in the chocolate chips in the mint chocolate chip ice cream we'd had for dessert. Who can say for sure? Once inside the car and heading south on I-95 toward Massachusetts, Dora screamed bloody murder for forty-five minutes before dropping into a coma-like slumber. George—patiently waiting until his sister had fallen silent—really perked up at the Piscataquis River Bridge (which separates Maine from New Hampshire) and managed to evade shut-eye for the next five hours by providing a running narrative of each sight, thought, and noise that entered his scope. This was particularly unnerving during the two-hour traffic jam we endured on 93 South, just outside of Boston.

Sometime after midnight, we crossed the Sagamore Bridge and shortly thereafter arrived at my parents' quaint and meticulously decorated colonial-era home. My folks were asleep in their bedroom on the first floor, and we had the run of the bedrooms on the second floor, where the various bed shapes and sizes presented George with the opportunity to whirl about, trying out each bed and deliberating on its pros and cons before collapsing prostrate in the middle of the king-size four-poster in the "master" guest room.

After strategizing about which of the remaining bed and room configurations would afford us the least disturbed sleep, Craig assumed the fetal position in bed next to George, and I jackknifed myself between Dora and the wall on a bed in an adjoining room.

The next morning, after a quick breakfast, Craig and I said our good-byes while Dora wailed and hung on to me like Julia Butterfly Hill on a redwood. My parents had managed to tranquilize George successfully by clicking the television over to Nickelodeon; he sat on the big couch, catatonically watching an episode of *SpongeBob SquarePants* without even noticing our departure. He was unable to tear his unblinking eyes from the hypnotizing power of the TV screen, even when I bent over him and lifted his chin up for a kiss.

And so we departed.

See, my hubby and I hadn't been away together (alone) for an overnight in three and a half years. And that particular overnight had preceded Dora's birth by exactly nine months. So at first, we were a little awkward with each other. It was sort of like a first date (fishing about for topics of conversation that engage and stimulate)—only with eleven years of baggage tacked on (fishing about for topics of conversation that won't enrage or alienate).

The backseat of our car was eerily silent—and so devoid of little mouths and feet and arms. The spots where the kids' car seats had once rested resembled a crime scene: pristine rectangles ringed with the detritus of childhood—broken crayons, popcorn, stickers, straws, deflated balloons, cookie crumbs, and action figurines.

We drove through the Cape's biceps and headed for the fist, reaching Provincetown just as the morning fog was burning off. And was it a scorcher! We decided to go to the beach, but then I realized that in my haste to pack I'd forgotten my bathing suit.

No, that's not true. I had neglected to pack my bathing suit because I looked like hell in it. I'd purchased the thing the previous fall, when I'd deluded myself enough to think that, come summer, I'd be magically transformed into one hot mama who could sport a bikini top connected to the high-cut bottoms with a piece of sultry black mesh.

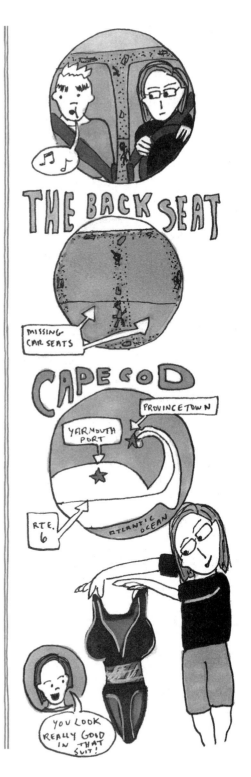

What the hell was I thinking? On the two occasions that I had dared to wear it thus far, I spent the time fruitlessly stuffing my boobs back into the top, pulling the wedgie out of my butt, and fending off George, who'd been weaned for four years but suddenly had renewed interest in my mammaries.

So we parked the car near our lodgings and sallied forth into bustling P-town in search of a bathing suit that would pleasingly adorn my post-childbearing form.

A lot had changed in the eleven years since Craig and I had tied the knot in this Portuguese fishing hamlet/gay summertime mecca: We'd had two kids, Craig's hair had turned white, my rear had (at least) doubled in size, and gay folks were flocking in droves to Provincetown to get married. Gone was the wacky, wild, cruisey, thumping pulse of yesteryear. In its place: pedicures, oxygen treatments, long naps, and mineral water . . . all leading up to the "I dos."

Plus, there were a whole lotta nerdy- and geeky-looking gay guys in P-town this time around—and a dearth of the super-hunky shirtless beefcakes I used to drool over in days gone by. Sure, I admit it: I like to watch a nice piece of taut male ass just as much as the next gal. But this particular year's parade of cycling helmets, paunchy middle-aged guts, hairy backs, and tiny mustaches left this hausfrau sorely disappointed.

After our anticlimactic oxygen treatment (we paid $30 for fifteen minutes of breathing, and though I did feel slightly more clearheaded afterward, I quickly nullified the effects by drinking several glasses of wine and then bumming a cigarette at a nearby bistro), we resumed our search for a bathing suit I could wear with confidence.

And we found one—or so I thought: black surfing shorts with white piping (so Jackie O!) and a matching tankini-esque top, which was rendered unmatronly by tying behind the neck, like a halter. But when I entered the dressing room and closed the curtain behind me, the mirror told another story. Even though I'd selected a size "L" from the rack, I couldn't even pull those frigging surfing shorts over my hips! And I thought, If my ass isn't "L," then what is it?

When I emerged, sweaty and befuddled, to a throng of gay men and my husband waiting anxiously, the diplomatic young man running the shop tried to appease me by stating that the surfing shorts were "Brazilian"—and thus, I shouldn't take it personally because Brazilian gals are so much smaller than we behemoth Americans. But I could not be soothed. I was stunned and repulsed by the body I was currently inhabiting. Where was my old body? I liked that one! And I wanted it back, pronto!

On our way out of the shop, I made a self-deprecating wisecrack (see bottom right) that the young, fit salesclerk—and all of the other lithe men who were hanging around the counter gossiping with him—found to be hilarious.

Back outside, we resumed our search amid all the folk who were serenely promenading down Commercial Street holding hands. After many fruitless dressing-room debacles, we abandoned all hope that I would don a bathing suit in P-town. Through sheer repetitive humiliation in boutique dressing rooms on the tip o' Cape Cod, I began to let go and accept the changes my body had endured in the past decade. I realized that the right bathing suit would present itself to me eventually, as long as I humbly kept the channels open and relaxed into my present-day role as a schlubby hausfrau from Maine who doesn't need a pair of Brazilian surfing shorts to make herself feel complete.

My man and I made our way back to our spacious ocean-view room at the Masthead, where we were staying, took showers, and called the kids. We then sat out on the Masthead's deck, and—feasting on wine, bread, cheese, and olives—began to sink into a comfortable flow of real conversation. We laughed together. We looked out over Cape Cod Bay. And as the sun set over Massachusetts, we spotted the very place we had said our vows eleven years before.

As we waxed philosophical about the changing tides of our lives, a tiny bird fluttered down and landed at our feet. He cocked his head quizzically for a moment, as if he were trying to make sense out of what we were saying, and then he proceeded to peck at our crumbs.

Five: Every Stick a Gun

very Stick a Gun! would be the
title of the miniseries that the Fox Network would
make about my son's life thus far.

Lookit: I'm a peace-lovin' mama. I've practiced "attachment parenting" ever since my son emerged from the womb. Violent toys, TV shows, and computer games are not welcome in our home. And so, when my sweet boy—at the age of two—began to show an interest in weaponry, I was startled and dismayed.

One morning at breakfast, he bit his toast into the shape of a gun. I didn't think much of it, but then he pointed it at my head and pulled the little toast trigger.

I searched for answers. How on Earth could a two-year-old boy know about guns? Was it part of the masculine cosmic unconscious?

As the oldest of three girls, I just cannot understand it. Guns were not a part of my childhood. I've theorized that perhaps George saw a movie-promo poster at Videoport when I took him there to rent a Thomas the Tank Engine movie or something. But whatever the culprit or cause of this fixation, we've been off and running ever since, in a frenzy of gun-toting war play and an obsession with weaponry of all kinds, including swords, cannons, spears, lances, missiles, maces, and nunchucks.

I go back and forth on the issue. Sometimes I think it's fine that my son is working out his stuff through imaginative play. After all, isn't making guns 'n' ammo out of items found in nature a creative act?

But then, sometimes I worry. One summer, George became fixated on an enormous piece of driftwood he found at Kettle Cove Beach. He would haul it onto his shoulder and shout at me to look at his "WMD," much to the consternation of nearby beachgoers. If I ignored him, it only served to inflame his passion. When I'd look up at him, he'd jump off the bridge by the little stream and take a dive into the dunes, spraying sand, his WMD flying. The sound effects he made—of grenades exploding and heavy artillery being fired— were quite impressive.

Sometimes I wonder whether my child is normal or if Craig and I have spawned some sort of gun-obsessed psychopath. I've discussed it with random men I've met—in line at the grocery store, for example, a place where George typically feels entitled to create a disturbance—and they all smile in recognition, nod their heads yes, and say that they were *just like that* as a boy and it's totally normal—and see! they didn't grow up to be serial killers, no sir, here they are in line at the grocery store, buying stuff.

And that makes me feel better.[1]

So do the times when George forgets about sticks and guns altogether and does things like run off and pick me a bouquet of wildflowers and then present his gift to me, as if he were milord and I his lady.

---

1. Except for that time the guy in front of us, who'd just validated George's behavior, went on to purchase a can of Crisco, some condoms, and a Valu-Pack of rubber bands.

Six: How It Came to Be that I Disposed of a Desiccated Robin, a Basketful of Caterpillars, and a Fried Mouse in One Long Weekend

n **Memorial Day weekend, our** family set out to spend the holiday on the shores of New Hampshire's Lake Winnepocket, where Craig's father owns a cottage. We're responsible for opening the cottage each spring, which entails turning on the utilities, scrubbing the place down, and then discovering and dealing with miscellaneous debris and animals that overwintered in the uninsulated house.

This year, we hit the jackpot. In addition to all the typical opening-day finds, we also discovered some wildlife that—well, wasn't "wild" or "alive" anymore.

When we arrived at the cottage after our three-hour drive, we sent the kids down to the beach to explore and play in the treasure trove of nature (no one puts a toe in the water without an adult present, mind you) so that Craig and I could commence the opening process. This scheme lasted a few minutes. The kids were attacked by clouds of blackflies and skeeters, so they tramped back into the house to "help" with cleaning and the laying out of provisions.

Meanwhile, as I was washing the windows, I kept noticing white splotches that looked like paint all over the floors 'neath each windowsill. Using my uncanny hausfrauian powers of deduction, I theorized that the splotches were not paint but bird poop—and that it appeared as if some wretched feathered friend had been frantically trying to get the hell out of the cottage at some point in the last eight months.

I announced my findings to the family, and Craig—in a moment of parenting genius—upped the ante. With monetary incentive, it took George about two nanoseconds to track the feather-and-poop trail and locate the poor dead thing under the bunk bed. He alerted us by whooping, "Dead bird! Under bed!" and then immediately demanded compensation for his services.

The deceased bird had been a robin, and we all paused for a moment of reflection. And then all eyes turned to me. Of course I had been silently nominated on the spot—as I always am—to deal with all things foul, putrid, and/or decaying. Around here, it's gender roles be damned!

I accepted my lot, found a section of *The New York Times* from a summer gone by, and slithered under the bunk. Once I'd scooped the robin up, Dora volunteered to help me bury it, and we females headed out the back door.

We found a shovel and I dug a grave,[1] and then, as the sun so appropriately began to sink behind Mount Kearsarge, at the top of the lake, we said our good-byes to the birdie. Dora got really quiet and her eyes welled up with tears, and then she delivered a eulogy that soundly wrenched this hausfrau's heart. I covered the dead bird with earth. And after a few bittersweet moments, we returned to the cottage to disinfect the site of death and scrub bird poop off the floors.

---

1. Yes, it was shallow. I admit it.

The next morning, we awoke to a cloudless sky and a wonderful breeze that blew down the mountain and over the lake and kept the bugs away. Hooray! Since we'd finished most of our chores the previous evening, we decided to take advantage of the perfect weather and spend the day enjoying the great outdoors. We swam, played ball on the beach, climbed Mount Kearsarge, and generally romped and frolicked all day long.

The bliss-fest came to a screeching halt, though, when we stopped at the grocery store on the way back from the mountain, and George suddenly remembered what he was owed. After suffering much embarrassment in the checkout line, Craig finally forked over the dough, and George piped down. He bought a Harry Potter movie-promo magazine with his payment. The outburst prompted us to beat it back to the cottage, and as we drove home, we unknowingly hurtled toward more dead critters.

At the lake, Craig began dinner prep. Dora napped. George fished. And I took the opportunity to meander around outside, smelling the lake smell and enjoying the flora. Then I noticed that one of the trees in front of the cottage had become home to an enormous gypsy moth caterpillar tent—and its voracious inhabitants were killing the tree. I hadn't seen a caterpillar tent this big since I was a kid and my hometown was plagued by the critters—so much so that when I used to walk in the woods behind our house, it sounded like it was raining from all the caterpillar turds dropping from the defoliated trees. My friend Joanne and I used to scrape caterpillars off the trees by the thousands, scorching them with lighters we'd swiped from our parents.

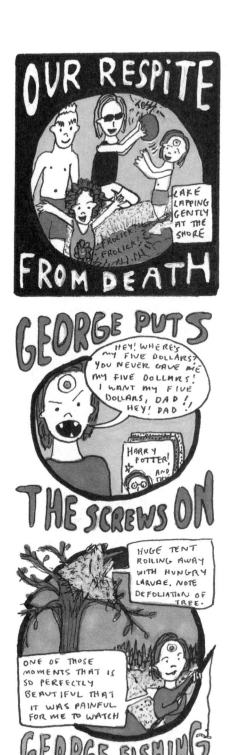

Anyhoo, I now took it upon myself to save the seriously munched-on tree—without resorting to toxic chemical sprays. I found a basket and a stick and then scooped the entire tent into the basket, thinking I was being ecologically minded by offering the larvae to George for use as bait in his fishing exploits. He took one look at the roiling mass in the basket and quickly rejected my plan. And boy, I didn't blame him! We put our ears up to the basket and the hundreds of caterpillars squirming around inside made a sound akin to meat sizzling on a griddle. Eeeeew!

George suggested that we build a fire and burn the critters, and even though I had done that very thing when I was a child, I decided that now, as a parent, I should model compassion and turn this into a learning moment. I initiated a discussion about karma, which failed miserably, George quickly pointing out the hypocrisy of my argument. I decided that we should drop the critters in the lake, reasoning that drowning them would be less karmically damaging than burning them.

I dumped the basket into the lake, and George and I sat at the end of the dock and watched to see if the fish would eat the caterpillars. There weren't any takers. The caterpillars sank to the bottom of the lake, and as the sun set, we were attacked by mosquitoes.

Our woodsy interlude was interrupted by a shriek from the cottage. We ran inside to find that while Craig had been making dinner, the electric stove had failed, and so he had pulled the appliance away from the wall to inspect the wiring in back. What he'd discovered was that a mouse had bitten into one of the stove's big black wires and had thus received a walloping jolt of electricity. The tiny creature was still attached to the frayed wire—by its teeth—and guess whose job it was to remove the crispy rodent carcass dangling from the back of the stove and dispose of it in the ever-growing lakeside critter graveyard? You guessed it! And so I did just that.

Sometime later that evening, after a delicious grilled dinner, we all sat around the fireplace, playing the board game Uncle Wiggily and reflecting on life's great mystery.

Seven: How It Came to Be that I Scraped Egg Residue Off the Walls of My Father-in-Law's Cottage

MOUNTAIN OF LAUNDRY (DRAWN TO SCALE)

"SITTING" ON MACHINE

I WANNA PUT DA MONEY IN! AND PUSH ALL DA BUTTONS!

HEY! WHAT ABOUT ME? I WANT TO PUT THE MONEY IN TOO!

Bush Cheney '04

"CHILDREN" ARE NOT ALLOWED TO "SIT" ON THE MACHINES! — THE "MGMT"

One morning later that summer, during our vacation at my father-in-law's cottage, Craig got up early and went back to our house in Portland to meet with some contractors about our leaking roof, and the kids and I decided to venture into town to poke around the shops and launder our heaping pile of dirty bedding, damp towels, and sandy, smeary, food-encrusted clothes.

It was at the Warner Laundr-O-Mat that we met the wrath of the Furious Laundr-O-Mat Proprietor.

Dora was itching to place our quarters into the washing-machine slots and then press the "start" buttons, and the only way her toddler obsession with all things mechanical could be satisfied was for me to lift her up on top of the machines, where all the slots and buttons live. This was the first of several hausfrauian acts in direct violation of the Furious Laundr-O-Mat Proprietor's Code of Ethics, which he had taken great pains to copy down onto oak tag signs with big, fat red and black Magic Markers and post in strategic locations throughout his emporium of cleanliness. But because I am such a harried hausfrau and was focusing only on shoving loads of dirty laundry into the Kenmores' maws, and also because at the time I was suffering from PMS-induced psychosis, I never noticed a thing.

And when the kids and I returned from the Toys in the Attic toy store thirty-two minutes later (an account

of which follows) to put our laundry into the dryer, the Furious Laundr-O-Mat Proprietor, who had apparently been spying on us from his lair in back of the dry-cleaning drop-off area, had removed all of our items from the washing machines, had piled them into two utility carts, and was presently standing in the middle of the floor, which was completely devoid of customers (except for us). So powerful was his rage that he was rendered speechless and could only point at his hand-made signs, on which he had taken huge grammatical liberties with quotation marks.

I suppose I could have argued with the jowly old fart that his quotation marks had confused me, since they lent such an ironic tone to the signs. Instead, I chose to remain silent and let him feel morally superior while he repeatedly pointed his withered index finger at his signs. I fantasized, meanwhile, about strangling the foul geezer with his Bush/Cheney '04 T-shirt.

The new toy store in town, conveniently located a block away from the Warner Laundr-O-Mat, was called Toys in the Attic. From the outside, Toys in the Attic promised a carefree romp through toy land, so the kids and I entered expecting to see kites 'n' fairies and the like. But what we discovered at this seriously mis-named establishment was that the toy store was actually a front for a geriatric anxiety festival, complete with a proprietress who followed us around the cramped shop, demanding that my children immediately put back every object that they picked up.

When George, for example, began to investigate a roll of wrapping paper that had been stocked in a large bin on the floor in front of the cash register, she swooped on him like a hawk. Apparently, all the toys and art supplies and glittery doodads and trinkets displayed at child's eye level were only for show.

The anxious proprietress led us into the "children's play area," a dingy, unlit closet at the back of the store, saying, "The children can play in here," before turning on her heel to go and nag some other poor child who had wandered in and was touching the rubber stamps. My kids made the best of it—God love 'em—sitting in the dungeon and attempting to build a structure with the smattering of Legos George found in a yellow bin.

I took this opportunity to check out the barrette display, as it had become my recent quest to find a way to keep Dora's wild locks out of her eyes. In order to make my scheme work, however, I needed Dora's buy-in, so I went and fetched her from the dungeon and set her up on the counter so she could get a good look at the barrettes. She chose a pair of $5 bumblebees, which I quickly paid for and popped into her tresses, not quite taming the tangled mass of curls as I had hoped.

At this point, the proprietress completely transformed and began to gush profusely about my daughter's physical appearance, head full of curly locks, and resemblance to Shirley Temple, and she kept singing "On the Good Ship Lollipop," which I found to be more unsettling than her obsessive focus on order-above-all-else. I helped the kids put the handful of Legos away, making sure to passive-aggressively leave several of them on the dungeon floor. And as we left through the tinkling door of Toys in the Attic, George, in his infinite wisdom, turned to me and summed up the situation perfectly.

After our encounter with the Furious Laundr-O-Mat Proprietor, we had twenty minutes of dryer time to kill, so we sought refuge at MainStreet BookEnds, a haven of good reading and quality, age-appropriate toys, which the kids could not only touch but also play with. As I heaved a sigh of relief and sat down on the floor to read a pirate book that George had selected, my head cleared for perhaps the first time that day, and I began to free-associate. And then I had the most horrifying realization: In my PMS-ing whirl to get us and our laundry out of the house that morning, I'd forgotten to shut off the front burner of the stove, which was therefore currently boiling away a pot of water that contained the eight (very) hard-boiled eggs that were to be our lunch.

I shrieked and grabbed Dora, who was at my feet dismantling one of her bumblebee barrettes, and yelled to George to come along pronto, and we jumped in the Subaru and raced back to the cottage. Even though I drove on the windy back-country roads with the pedal to the metal, it was still a nightmarishly slow, nail-chomping fifteen-minute car ride, and of course my mind clamped down on the worst possible scenario: my father-in-law's house would have burned to the ground in the last two hours, and I would arrive at the lake just in time to watch the last structural beam collapse onto the heap of smoldering wreckage.

But, ah—sweet relief! The house was still miraculously standing when we pulled into the driveway, and the only evidence of my forgetfulness was a truly amazing explosion of charred egg residue covering every surface in the kitchen.

Later that evening, after Craig returned from Portland and we'd eaten dinner, I got down to business scraping the egg off the walls and cupboards with a spatula, while the kids and my hubby played Uncle Wiggily beside the fire. I was grateful to the parenting gods. And all was well.

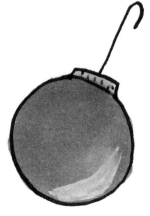

Eight: Hausfrau Holiday Bake-off, or Another Portrait Norman Rockwell Forgot to Paint

got it stuck in my craw one holiday season to create a cheery yuletide glow in our home by making Christmas cookies.[1] There's a problem, though, I've found, with having any warm 'n' fuzzy expectations when it comes to my kids.

It's not that we don't have warm 'n' fuzzy moments. We do. And they always take my breath away: so beautiful, so intimate, so real.

But these moments are usually unexpected and cannot be created by my force of will.

And still, my fantasies persist!

Anyhoo, one Saturday morning before Christmas, when Craig was away at a conference for nonprofit organizations, the kids and I arose and—like little elves in Santa's workshop—set to work after a light breakfast. And that's when mama's warm 'n' fuzzy cookie-making fantasy was abruptly shattered, like an icicle dropping off the roof of a three-story building.

---

1. Actually, it happened like this: Once again, I completely missed the point (that it's all about the cookie-making *process* and the joy of giving) and decided to make the cookies in the first place because our tenant, Taurus, shoveled out our driveway during a snowstorm, and I felt so guilt-ridden about the fact that Craig was absent and I had been sleeping while a single mom performed our chores for us that I concocted the cookie scheme as a way to repay her and thus assuage my guilt.

My children fought over each step, each ingredient, and each utensil, so that I was forced to attempt to split everything exactly in half—and I'm talking down to the molecular level, because if one of them got a molecule more salt (that's NaCl), for example, all hell would break loose. The screaming and scratching and shoving and slapping and crying went on and on, and even though it was not yet noon, I craved the sweet, easy escape that a couple of mugs of spiced eggnog and a set of earplugs would afford me.

Neither of these items were at the ready, however, and so my nerves continued to wear down like a piece of fresh ginger rubbed vigorously against a cheese grater, while Dora and George found new unmet needs and disparities to explore and complain loudly about. At one point I put on a Christmas music CD, which my sister Boo had made for us,[2] but my attempt to soothe/distract my little cherubs with the calming power of music failed miserably, as they then began to argue about which track we should listen to.

Soon, Dora noticed the bowl of sanding sugar on the counter, and when I turned around from the sink, both she and her brother were dipping their fingers into the bowl and licking the sugar off, like tiny coke addicts huddled over a mirror.

---

2. Containing such excellent tunes as Rickie Lee Jones's rendition of "Silent Night" and The Beach Boys' rockin' good "Little Saint Nick."

In my desperation, and because the kitchen was now quiet (save for the sound of little teeth crunching down on sugar granules and the occasional grunt), I ignored them for a few moments and breathed in the delicious silence. This, in retrospect, was tantamount to relaxing in the few dead-calm moments before an F-5 tornado descends upon your trailer.

Perhaps I should have clued in to the fact that it was almost lunchtime. Perhaps I should have offered some healthy food choices to my kids, since a truly tuned-in hausfrau would have recognized her children's misbehavior as a plea for protein-based nourishment. It doesn't matter, because my negligence was duly punished by the parenting gods: Those five minutes of blissful silence were followed by several hours of the worst hyperactivity I'd witnessed since George ate an entire cloud of cotton candy at the Cumberland County Fair.

My son lost interest in cookie-making altogether and found an activity more in line with his blood/sugar ratio: diving repeatedly onto the mammoth pile of clean laundry I'd left on our bed to fold later.[3]

Dora stuck with our project, but only in hopes of gaining access to more sugar, and she kept climbing up on the counter to get at it. The crowning moment came when she sneezed into the cookie batter. I decided at that point that we were through with our experiment in homemade baked goods.

---

3. I had been hoping, of course, that someone else—such as, hmmm . . . a kindly elf, or perhaps maybe even my hubby—would fold the clothes for me.

I put the remainder of our germ-infested dough into the fridge and whisked the kids over to the children's museum, where I could at least jibber-jabber with other hausfraus while the children worked off their sugar highs by hurling large Styrofoam blocks at each other and clanging the fire engine bell and jumping off the rainbow bridge onto the floor below.

I saw my friend "Dr. M" at the museum, and while she nursed her newborn son, Sam, we chatted. I casually tried to work in a question about whether the heat of my oven would be sufficient to kill off a virus. Dr. M's answer was hugely relieving to me and gave me just enough hope to be able to face the next several hours.

I drove home and finished the cookie project that evening after dinner with the kids, who were by that time nourished and therefore focused and loving me and each other and our project, reminding me yet again that it isn't all about me. It's really hardly ever about me.

After dinner, we went downstairs to deliver the guilt-assuaging, dead-virus-laden cookies to Taurus and Tammy and Reggie, but they weren't at home and were in fact gone for the holidays. So we brought the whole plate of cookies back upstairs and ended up eating them by ourselves with lots of milk before bed. And boy, were they delicious.

Nine: I'm Not Kathy! My Name Is Mommy!

Apparently, I'm turning out to be a big flippin' disappointment to my daughter. This point was illustrated to me yet again this morning, as I attempted to flip the Arthur[1] pancake she'd crafted in the skillet. As I raised the spatula underneath Arthur's "face," the "ears" gave way and broke off. And let me tell you, there was HELL to pay! Dora, who'd been perched right next to me atop a stool, where she'd been scrutinizing my every move, threw her head back and wailed at me for my oafish lack of dexterity. Hissy fit number one went on and on as I worked furiously to repair the damage. I was at last successful in patching Arthur's ears back on to his multigrain noggin.

But then, just moments later, I incurred the wrath of my daughter yet again by mistakenly pouring honey onto her prized pancake, rather than the syrup that she desired.

---

1. The rendering at left is what Arthur™ looks like, for those of you not hip to PBS Kids programming. Arthur, I have learned, is supposed to be an aardvark. But will somebody please tell me, for the love of God, how that can be so? Don't aardvarks have long proboscises that they use to suck ants out of the ground? Or is that an anteater? In any case, Dora's pancake looked more like an aardvark than Arthur™ does, if you ask me.

She screamed and howled at me, and even though I was able to remedy my gross and unforgivable error by scraping the honey off the pancake and offering her the syrup, Dora progressed into hissy fit number two—inconsolable.

But then I mentioned that it was time to get ready for dance class with *KATHY*, a four-year-old girl's dream-come-true.

Who is this *KATHY* and what kind of a magic hold does she have on my daughter?

KATHY is a truly gifted dance teacher, whom Delia told me about when Dora started dancin' up a storm around the house. *KATHY* let us sit in on a class, and Dora was hooked immediately. And what young lady in her right mind wouldn't be? The girls get to dress up in tutus and sparkly shoes and gloves and sprinkle "fairy dust" all over themselves, and play and dance with fairy dolls that *KATHY* hides in a tiny tree, and dance with scarves and pretend that they're snowflakes and kittens and Dorothy from *The Wizard of Oz* as they skip around, unfettered and encouraged, looking at themselves in the wall-to-wall mirrors and eating chocolate chip cookies that *KATHY* baked herself. It is forty-five minutes of four-year-old-girl bliss that is joyful and under control and pure magic to behold!

Each week I sit in the parents' viewing area, tears welling up in my eyes as I watch my daughter's inner light receive a supercharge, and I am filled with love and joy and gratitude to *KATHY*, but I also have a twinge of sadness that feels like part of my heart has managed to burst out of my chest and is currently twirling around on the dance floor.

Because even though I like to cut a rug as much as the next gal, I'm not filled with endless exuberance, patience, and creativity, and I'm not always in the mood to crank up the tunes and pretend that I'm the Sugar Plum Fairy whenever Dora asks me to. I wish I were. I wish I were more . . . what? Fun? Lighthearted? Dainty of step and dexterous of hand? Nimble of finger? Thinner? I guess I wish I could feel a little lighter. A little freer. A little more like *KATHY*.

So then tonight I'm in the kitchen, making dinner, and Dora is dancing in the living room to *The Nutcracker*. She's got her fairy wings on and her tiara and the pink sparkly shoes that Uncle Tom and Aunt Cindy gave her for her fourth birthday, which she hasn't taken off since, and she calls out to me to come dance with her, and I say I can't because I'm making dinner. And then after the Sugar Plum Fairy number ends, she comes into the kitchen and explains to me that she loves *KATHY* very, very much and gives me the rundown on the scale she has created for gauging her love. I stand there, smiling and holding the information she's just shared inside, where it hurts really bad.[3]

But then my daughter skips off again, and I take a big breath and break out the goods and pour myself a nice big glass o' wine. Ah, motherhood! Cheers!

2. What Would *KATHY* Do?

3. A sensation akin to being stabbed in the heart with a railroad spike.

Ten: My M.I.A. Libido

ver the winter, my libido hit a nadir that was inversely related to the height of the ever-growing mountain of snow behind the Wild Oats parking lot.[1]

I think I might have S.A.D. (that's seasonal affective disorder, for those of you in climes less brutal and punishing than ours here on the salty and rugged Maine coast, where in winter the sun reaches a taunting slant for a few hours each day before dropping out of sight beyond the horizon—which means that the brain cells responsible for producing feelings of well-being when stimulated by UV light clock out sometime toward the end of October). Thus, the lack of sunlight, frigid temperatures, and record-breaking snowfall began to take their toll on me around the first week of January, after the hustle and bustle of Hanukkah and the Christmas holidays and New Year's was over.

---

1. Explanation for those "from away": We here in Portland had received such a walloping amount of snow that we broke all manner of records and the city had no idea what to do with all of the white stuff accumulating on our streets and parking lots. So they decided to load it into dump trucks and deposit it in a two-city-block-by-two-city-block space behind Wild Oats, my frequent trips to which became occasions for George to ogle the mounting pile and fantasize about his eventual ascent.

2. I pretty much lifted this speech from Jonathan Edwards's "Sinners in the Hands of an Angry God" (Boston, 1741) and added a few seasonally appropriate *bons mots* of my own.

Why, you ask, don't we uproot the family and move to a more hospitable climate—or at least buy one of those UV-light boxes? It's because I come from a long line of stubborn Yankees who tell ourselves that we belong here because the changing seasons remind us that without winter there would be no spring. But the truth is that we just really love our own misery. Because if you took that away, what would be left?

The ghost of my Puritan Forefather was with me constantly—making sure to admonish me whenever I attempted to sneak in a moment of pleasure for myself—while outside the winter wind howled.

And can you blame me for seeking a temporary hiatus—albeit in a bottle? The parade of sour-faced New Englanders (and I include myself in that parade) had pushed me to the breaking point. I developed a cozy relationship with anything I could get my hands on that made me feel warm and satisfied—even if it was momentary. And illusory. And expensive.

Even so, the wine didn't suffice to warm me up enough to want to get it on with my man.

But my pint-size libido was the least of my worries. Just getting out of the driveway in the morning became a several-hour process, and shoveling away another heavy layer of snow while dodging my son's snowball assault was just the beginning.

Of course, just like the helpful Ingalls children in the *Little House* series, which we were currently reading together, my son sought out every opportunity to assist his "ma."

For roughly the same reasons as those cited in my explanation of why I haven't purchased a UV-light box, I also insisted on shoveling the driveway after each storm pummeled us, complaining all the while and publicly disparaging the man next door who easily removed the snow from his family's driveway with his snowblower, which I secretly lusted after with mounting intensity after every nor'easter.

Lucky for us, my father-in-law sprang for an all-expenses-paid family reunion on the tropical isle of Puerto Rico in mid-February, and the promise of Caribbean temps and rum drinks helped keep me at least partially hinged through the first half of the winter. We escaped Portland at 4:30 in the morning, amid yet another blinding snowstorm, and landed on San Juan's welcoming tarmac approximately nine hours later.

3. During the snow-removal portion of our winter days, Dora usually opted to stay inside but would press her face against the living-room window and scream for me to stop shoveling and come inside. I worried that Taurus would call DHS.

Lemme tell ya: The fragrant, balmy breezes that hit us as we deplaned were more delicious and intoxicating than any alcoholic concoction—although I did manage to knock back my fair share of 'em with my sister-in-law, Elisa, as we lounged at the truly decadent hotel bar, which was partially submerged in the pool so that you could get good 'n' soused without ever having to haul your tired and flabby arse out of the water. Ah, American ease and comfort on such a tiny commonwealth of an isle!

I was shocked and dismayed to find, however, that Elisa had deceived me. During a phone conversation the week before our trip, she'd led me to believe that she, too, had put on quite a bit of extra poundage since we'd last seen each other. We joked together about muumuus and large aquatic mammals, and I felt relieved that I would not be alone in my "largesse." So of course she arrived looking rail-thin and well-kempt, and when we stood next to each other for photo ops, we resembled the before and after photos for diet pills that you can find in the back of certain magazines.

But really, it felt so damn good to be warm for a few days and walk barefoot on the tropical beaches and swim in the surf (the temperature of which I would have to describe as "tepid"[4]) and stimulate my optic nerves with lots of natural UV light that I was able to forgive my sister-in-law for her breach of solidarity and even forget about my unsightly thighs 'n' saggy boobs and settle into a really excellent four days.

---

4. Swimming in warm ocean water was, for us, a novelty. In Maine, one does not "swim" in the ocean, but rather visits it for a few anus-clenching seconds in order to "cool off" during August heat waves.

George and I bodysurfed for hours. We watched lizards that scampered around like chipmunks. We treated ourselves to ice cream every night in the hotel lobby. And Craig got to smoke some really good Cuban cigars and bond with his dad.

I think my shrunken, grinchy heart grew at least two sizes. But not my libido.

Upon our return to Portland, we found that two and a half feet of wet, heavy snow had been deposited in our driveway, and unlike my hubby and children, who seemed to have been refreshed and rejuvenated by our mini-vacation and were ready to cope with another two-plus months of the deep freeze, I grew despondent as I relocated each shovelful of the white stuff. I began to view our tropical getaway not as a recharging break but more as a climate-based tease, and one that had left me with a nasty case of blue balls.

But since I never allow myself to stop and feel the grief, I pushed onward and plunged our family into a brand-new adventure.

We got home, shoveled the driveway, put our summer clothes back into storage, where they'd remain for the next four and a half months, and then put on our woolens and winter boots and headed out to Turkey Hill, to watch the farm for our friends John, Stacy, and Emma, while they were away in Oaxaca, Mexico, and to take care of their dog and a bunch of cats and twenty or so chickens. And a rooster.

The rooster was a total trip and finally answered for me the question of why the male genital member is referred to as a "cock." My libido might have been M.I.A., but Mr. Rooster's was present and accounted for, and this fact gave us ample opportunities for teaching the kinder about the natural world, and provided me with lots of material to write about in my journal.

The rooster! The rooster! What a fine and feathered beast! Whenever the kids and I went out to collect eggs from the coop, we saw the rooster routinely and joyously ramming the hell out of his female coop-mates. So taken was I with this feathered sex machine that I did some research on the Internet and unearthed the following:

Roosters are not necessary for the production of eggs, and hens do not lay better if one is present. In fact, production goes down if hens are injured during mating. The rooster's spurs and claws damage backs, and he commonly pulls out head feathers while trying to hold on. Hens low on the pecking order are more likely to submit to breeding and therefore suffer more broken feathers and scratching. The smaller the flock, the more likely these subordinate hens will suffer injuries from an aggressive rooster. Aldrovandi (a Renaissance naturalist) noted in 1600 that "the lustfulness of the rooster is recognized not only from the great frequency with which he copulates with his own wives but even more from the fact that if the hens are gone he does not in the slightest refrain from the males, but in the middle of the barnyard he mounts the one who has entered it most recently. . . . Children appreciate neither the aggression nor the amorous attentions of any rooster. The most common reason for a rooster to see the stew pot is his attacks on children.[5]

5. From *Organic Farms, Folks and Foods*, the quarterly newsletter of the Northeast Organic Farming Association of New York, Inc. (© 2005 by NOFA-NY).

Whoa nelly! Now I understood George's heretofore unexplainable and bizarre yet growing obsession with the rooster, which he named "Dynamite" and with which he was both fascinated and repulsed. Mostly, he enjoyed provoking the bird into attack mode, and would report back about his antics after spending four or five hours a day in the chicken coop. George also introduced many a playdate friend to Dynamite—and he and his cohorts romped for hours in the dust and feathers, while outside the coop, the snow continued to fall.

And then there were the barn cats. They were mere kittens but were already starting to go into heat, and the poor little things would roll around and stick up their behinds and mewl and howl as if being tormented. George emphatically condemned their behavior while nevertheless watching them with unflinching attention.

The barnyard antics did nothing for my libido. But something about that rooster sure jump-started George's fascination with all things sexual. One night at Videoport, where Craig had taken the kids to rent some movies, George disappeared while Craig was inquiring about the DVD release date for the third season of *Six Feet Under*. Craig searched for George in the aisles— and after several heart-pounding minutes, he finally made his way over to the "Adult" section of the store. Indeed, it was there that George had (innocently?) wandered, and when he noticed Craig's approach, he looked up from the video he was clutching and, with complete earnestness, registered his vote for the video selection du jour.

Craig and I decided that it was time for a little impromptu sex ed, so we borrowed a book called *It's Perfectly Normal* from some friends, and I took on the job of trying to connect with my son around the birds and the bees—to no avail. Like everything else, it seems, he needed to figure it out on his own terms. For now, anyway.

That was fine with me because I figured I needed to get a handle on my *own* deal and examine my M.I.A. libido, slice by frigid slice. And I began to wonder: Will the snow ever melt? Will the Hausfrau's desire ever awaken and unfurl?

Eleven: Apocalyptic Hausfrau, or How It Came to Be that My Head Nearly Exploded Whilst I Drove South on I-95 During a Deluge

few weeks after Hurricane Katrina, I drove down to visit my friend Ana[1] in Lincoln, Massachusetts, because she'd just given birth to a baby girl. Since it was a Friday, the kids were at school and I was alone for the two-hour drive: a fact I would normally relish for the rare, quiet solitude it would entail. But on this day there was rain—biblical rain; rain like the kind that Travis Bickle refers to in *Taxi Driver;* rain that was stripping all the foliage off the trees before we could appreciate the autumnal hues; rain that was causing rivers to swell mightily and wash away homes, cars, and picnic tables across New England; rain that made hydroplaning inevitable and had caused the fatal highway crashes of eight Mainers that week; rain that, when viewed through a lens that also took into view the tempests that had been pummeling the Gulf Coast, the subsequent flooding and destruction of the Big Easy, and the massive earthquake that had just struck Pakistan, had convinced me that the end of the world was nigh.

To top it off, I was listening to a call-in radio show on Boston's NPR affiliate, and the guest happened to be Simon Winchester, who was hawking his book *A Crack in the Edge of the World,* which is all about the 1906 earthquake that completely leveled San Francisco. He also spoke of the inevitability of the next massive Bay Area quake (aka, The Big One). Needless to say,

---

1. Chef extraordinaire of Oleana Restaurant in Cambridge, Massachusetts.

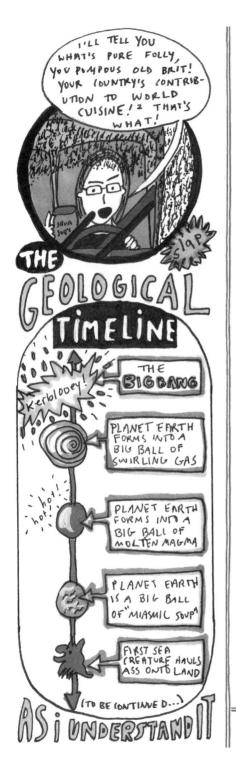

Mr. Winchester's emphatic prophecies—delivered in a clipped, snotty British accent—only served to exacerbate my mounting worries that Mother Nature was gearing up to shrug me, my family, and the rest of mankind offa this here planet. In my caffeine-induced panic, I tortured myself with horrible visions: that the apocalypse would happen while I was on my journey to visit Ana and her new babe, and we'd all be extinguished before I could get home to my family—and also that the final season of *Six Feet Under* was presently sitting in our DVD player, half-watched.

Mr. Winchester droned on and on, cataloging the cataclysms that have obliterated large cities and civilizations and so forth. And though I'll be the first to admit that I'm embarrassed as all get-out by the Administration-Which-Shall-Not-Be-Named and the disgusting mess we're making in Iraq and other locales around the globe, and have decided to disguise myself and my family as Canadians if we can ever scrape together enough dough to travel abroad, I felt a surge of patriotism and love for my motherland when Mr. Winchester implied that we were all a bunch of buffoons.

2. I stole this snappy comeback from Kevin Kline's character in the movie *A Fish Called Wanda*.

Even though I have argued that very same point countless times myself, I valiantly defended my country against his verbal onslaught—and did so aloud, in the car, in the pouring rain, to no one. I always feel compelled to argue with the radio, television, or newspaper when jacked up out of my gourd on caffeine—and this was no exception.

I drove and drove, and the rain poured harder, and then Mr. Winchester brought up the whole "geological timeline" concept—and all hell broke loose inside this here hausfrau's noggin. Whenever I've had the pleasure of someone demonstrating my meaninglessness to me in this way—my seventh grade science teacher, for example, who, in his office after school also introduced some of the girls in my class to the concept of pedophilia—it never fails to cause me many conflicting emotions simultaneously, including (but not limited to) panic, relief, comfort, distress, depression, elation, confusion, and clarity. As I drove, I pondered the vast expanse of eras and epochs and millennia of nothing but miasmic soup, trying to make sense of it all, trying to put this big stinkin' mess into some sort of context, trying to gain perspective on the increase in natural disasters that had been plaguing the world of late, and I realized that if I moved to Pennsylvania, I could relax completely because then I could pin it all on "intelligent design."

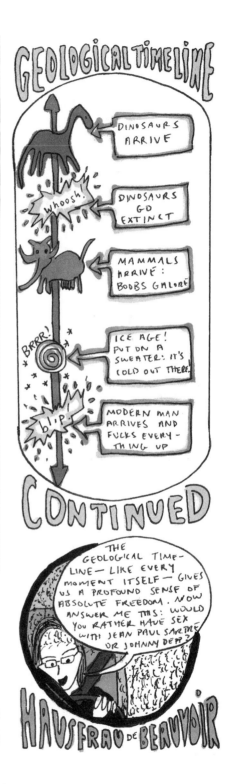

But that was not a possibility, because I was presently hurtling down Interstate 95 between Portland, Maine, and Boston in an apocalyptic rainstorm, wired to the teeth on the enormous travel mug[3] of French Roast I had just consumed.

So I did what any self-respecting hausfrau would do in that situation: I started wildly free-associating—my mind speeding through the decades—and I thought of my favorite San Francisco denizen, my dear friend John A. Vlahides. It was he who had introduced me to Ana, like twenty years ago now, after they'd returned from cooking school in Paris. Ana and I had hit it off immediately, and she had moved in to my amazing rent-controlled apartment in Cambridge near Harvard Square. Ah, those were the days! We were dewy and fresh-faced and the world was our oyster. It truly was the Age of Innocence.[4]

---

3. It was really more of a flagon.

4. Not to be confused with Edith Wharton's excellent novel and one of my favorite all-time reads about Manhattan's Victorian-era upper crust, nor with Martin Scorsese's very good movie-ization of that novel, starring Daniel Day-Lewis and Hollywood sweetheart-turned-shoplifter Winona Ryder, who, incidentally, broke the heart of Johnny Depp. And can I just interject into this narrative for a second to say that—his bewildering performance as Willy Wonka in Tim Burton's remake of *Charlie and the Chocolate Factory* notwithstanding—I would follow that man into the maw of hellfire and damnation any day of the week, and I believe that George would as well, given that he loved Johnny's Willy (Wonka, that is) and because ever since he and his friend Emma got to stay up late and watch *Pirates of the Caribbean,* his speech has been peppered with swashbuckling pirate-isms.

5. Check out the persuasive argument George presented to convince me to let him and Emma watch *Pirates of the Caribbean,* starring Johnny Depp.

Ah, the Age of Innocence! What a sweet and well-remembered time! It was 1990. Cigarettes were $3 a pack. I had no stretch marks. I'd just started dating Craig, and the only baggage that existed between us was his little duffel bag, which he packed with a contact-lens case and cleaning solution and a toothbrush and a change of clothes on the nights he'd stay over at my rent-controlled apartment. Craig was in a band called the El Caminos, and I was a loyal groupie, whose most profound thoughts involved what kind of cocktails I should order at the bars I frequented.

Flash forward, however, twenty years, and bear witness to the striking shifts in consciousness that have taken place in my caffeine-addled brain. I dunno, it seems like I've lost something *more* than my innocence since then. I've also lost the ability to process and file away all the information that constantly bombards me, so that it all swirls around while my synapses crackle and fizz. The protective sheaths around my dendrites have all worn away from a solid decade of drug- and alcohol abuse in the late eighties and early nineties, and so the neurons constantly misfire, like Cincinnati policemen.

When you add to that the constant worry about what my children will be facing as they come of age in this world, and *then* I drink a pot of coffee and get in a car set on a southerly course in a blindingly heavy rainstorm, and then some over-educated British guy starts yawping about the inevitable destruction of arguably the best city in America, and my fears of apocalypse are further exacerbated by the two phone conversations I had that morning, prior to my departure, which I previously forgot to mention—it's just a miracle my head didn't explode right then and there, sending blood and chunks o' gray matter and tufts of hair all over the windshield like a scene from a Quentin Tarantino movie. Instead, I was able to keep it all together, keep it all inside, keep on truckin', man, and even reached my destination only a few minutes late.

Ana welcomed me in out of the rain, which had begun to soften somewhat and was now more benign and soothing. I went straight for that beautiful new babe, Siena, who was sleeping peacefully in the quiet house. I cradled her in my arms and smelled her sweet head and rubbed my cheek against her peach fuzz and fell in love a little. And I thought, Maybe Craig and I should have another baby . . .

And then I thought, Why don't I just relax and enjoy this moment here. This one right now.

6. Note to self: Get a woodstove. Pronto.

7. Surely, I reasoned with Lynne, Paul Newman didn't utilize slavery in his chocolate-bar production. Right?

Twelve: The Unhip Mama

on't get me wrong. J mean in no way to slander or disparage the goddess Ariel Gore, founder of *Hip Mama* magazine and author of *The Mother Trip*, among many other books that tell the truth about motherhood and actually saved my sorry ass—along with Ayun Halliday's *The Big Rumpus* and her zine, *The East Village Inky*—by pulling me out of a mammoth depression/alienation festival way back in Y2K.[1] No, Ariel Gore has forever secured her spot in my pantheon of mother goddesses, and I bow down to her.

My wretched condition has nothing to do with Ariel Gore or *Hip Mama* but rather has manifested itself as a slow 'n' steady wearing away of this here hausfrau's hipness quotient, something I finally recognized when I attempted to consign a large L.L. Bean bag[2] full of my clothing and shoes at the very hip shop Material Objects, located on Congress Street in downtown Portland. I'd frequented Material Objects in the past, usually to purchase gifts or simply to drool over the wickedly cool shoes and clothing, the cute bags and stockings, as well as the jewelry and accessories arrayed on the walls and in the glass case in front of the cash register, where business is conducted.

---

1. Or, as I liked to call it, Y2GAY.

2. Here in Maine, we hausfraus can often be seen carrying stuff (in summer: snacks, sunscreen, wipes, bathing suits, towels, bottled water; in winter: skates, hats, mittens, snacks, bottled water, etc.) in these dorky yet indispensable canvas totes.

Dora always wanted to come with me so she could swing like a monkey from the clothing racks and beg loudly for jewelry and surprise the hip shoppers by peering 'neath the dressing room doors. Material Objects is a consignment store, but I had yet to consign my own clothing there, as I just never seemed to be able to get it together to mindfully go through my piles and boxes and huge black plastic trash bags bursting with outfits of yesteryear. For some inexplicable reason,[3] it was easier—albeit more painful[4]—for me to go through the boxes of clothes my children had worn as babies and give them away to the Goodwill on St. John Street or to new mamas. Jesus! What a scene! I would sit on the attic floor, sobbing uncontrollably, clutching 6-month-size snowsuits and yellow-diarrhea-stained onesies, trying to sniff that sweet milky essence of babe once again, now tinged with attic must.

But anyhoo, I finally was able to gather my confidence one night, while Craig was putting the kids to sleep, by drinking the lion's share of a bottle of wine and then pulling all my crap out of the attic and dumping it into a gargantuan pile on our bed.

---

3. Oh, wait. I can explain it. It's much easier to deal with other people's stuff than your own, n'est-ce pas?

4. Akin to tearing out my own fingernails with a pair of pliers.

I got down to business, carefully considering the hipness quotient of each article of clothing and footwear before separating it all into two piles:[5] the hip (i.e., a medium-size L.L. Bean bag of items bound for Material Objects) and the not hip (i.e., a towering heap of clothing bound for Goodwill). Granted, the Goodwill pile had to be loaded into two contractor-size plastic trash bags, but still, I thought that the carefully chosen Material Objects items represented a decent showing of post-childbearing hipness on my part. I was sadly mistaken.

On the day of my consignment appointment, Dora and I arrived at Material Objects at the designated time. I dropped the L.L. Bean bag full of presumably hip clothing off at the counter, whereupon it was taken by a very hip young woman into the back room (off limits to customers), where—I fantasized—the arbiter of hipness stood, looking something like Tina Turner, perhaps, clad in a black latex body stocking and platform boots, holding a whip aloft.

5. Actually, there were three piles. The third comprised items so disgraceful that I tossed them directly into the trash or under the kitchen sink, where our dust rags live. These included: a T-shirt from a local late-nineties nonprofit fund-raiser with an embarrassingly bad logo and a neck besmirched by multiple drips of hair-coloring product; once-hip black tights with a now-stretched-beyond-the-pale waistband, runs a plenty, and holes in the feet; and a lone, ill-fitting acrylic black sock, with an orange spiderweb pattern, which I think my mother got for me as a Halloween present at CVS.

6. Another excruciatingly difficult milestone, which involved painting over the choo-choo train mural in George's room that I had created for him as a surprise for his third birthday. I had to drink several glasses of wine before I could even wield the paint roller. The choo-choo train has since been replaced by a Boston Red Sox poster, but there have been other phases, many other phases, in the interim, including fire trucks, Buzz Lightyear, the Power Rangers, Batman, Spider-Man, rocket ships, Pokemon, *Magic* cards, drums, skateboarding, and *The Lord of the Rings*.

I thought that Dora and I would have ample time to walk down to Coffee by Design to get a latte to-go for me and a big cupcake with vanilla frosting and rainbow sprinkles for her, but before Dora had even finished swinging on one clothing rack, my L.L. Bean bag was back on the floor in front of the counter, and I was alerted that my consignment appointment was over.

Waiting until we got back to the car so I could paw through the bag in privacy to discern which, if any, articles had been chosen by the arbiter of hipness for acceptance into consignment at Material Objects, my mind was aswirl with questions. The bag looked exactly as full as it had been upon drop-off. Were any of my clothes hip enough for Material Objects? Apparently not. If the items I had thought were hip were deemed unhip by the arbiter of hipness, then what did that mean?

Luckily, I had my loving family to help me process the event that night around the dinner table.

---

7. How incestuous is Portland, Maine? Funny you should ask. "Dank" is Mike Dank, George's drum teacher and the banjo player in Poor Valley Salvation Society, Craig's current band. Jen is Dank's longtime partner and the co-owner of Material Objects.

8. My hubby's mild-mannered façade deceives. He's actually a much bigger gossip and is even cattier than I.

9. I told George that Bebe Buell is the mother of Liv Tyler, the actress who played Arwen, the elf princess, in the *Lord of the Rings* trilogy, his obsession du jour. Inappropriate to mention, I felt, was the fact that Bebe Buell is best known for her romantic liaisons with just about every male rocker of the seventies and eighties, which she chronicles in her gripping kiss-and-tell memoir, *Rebel Heart: An American Rock 'n' Roll Journey,* by Bebe Buell with Victor Bockris. I've prepared the CliffsNotes, at right, to provide a sense of the scope of "naughty" Bebe's career, but I recommend that you read the book in its entirety if you happen to relish gory details, like I do, such as the fact that Jimmy Page used to spit his saliva into Bebe's mouth when they kissed, and Jack Nicholson—the gross old pig—liked it when Bebe called him "Zeke" and once bonked her against a car with his pants around his ankles. Eeeeew!

CLIFFS NOTES
BUELL'S REBEL HEART

DANK + JEN

WHADDO I GOTTA DO TO GET MY CLOTHES CONSIGNED? SLEEP WITH MICK JAGGER?

★ BEFORE THE AGE OF 21: Bebe managed to do some modelling in NYC while maintaining a stormy relationship with Todd Rundgren and having flings with the likes of Jimmy Page of Led Zeppelin, Iggy Pop, David Bowie, and Mick Jagger.

★ ON HER 21st BIRTHDAY: John Lennon sang "Happy Birthday" to Bebe at a private bash in his NYC apartment!

★ AFTER THE AGE OF 21: Bebe poses for a Playboy centerfold, has a wild affair with a coked-up-beyond-belief Steven Tyler of Aerosmith and gets pregnant with his daughter (Liv Tyler) and also has sex with Rod Stewart (yuck!), Jack Nicholson, Warren Beatty, and Richard Butler of The Psychedelic Furs. She also carries on a sporadic + heartwrenching affair with Elvis Costello before "settling down" to make music, manage her daughter's career, and hang out with folks like Keith Richards, Debbie Harry, and Marianne Faithful.

CATTY HUBBY

MEOW.

And so, after my rejection from Material Objects, I told my tale of woe to everyone, including my Tuesday night proprioceptive writing[11] group. Their insightful comments and tales of their own humiliations buoyed me up considerably, especially Lynne's story about the time the Catholic Charities Refugee Resettlement Program rejected her donated futon.

---

10. The enthusiasm with which my son speaks of the beautiful elf princess Arwen is matched only by his adoration for his drum teacher, Mike Dank, whose teaching studio at the Drum Shop (at Union Station Plaza on St. John Street in Portland, right near the Goodwill) has, for our family, become a portal into another dimension. It is a dimension, it would seem, in which all the loose ends of our lives are tied to those of Mike Dank, so that our tiny universe here in Maine feels truly complete—but also sometimes a little eerie, a little *too* riddled with coincidence, like, for example, the fact that Mike Dank grew up a few blocks away from Craig in Cleveland, Ohio, and attended the same Jewish preschool there.

11. From the official proprioceptive writing website (www.pwriting. org): "Proprioceptive Writing (PW) is a method for exploring the psyche through writing. Easy enough for anyone to learn it, PW is practiced to music in 25-minute sessions, under stress-free conditions, alone or in groups. Through a process we call 'Inner Hearing,' PW teaches you to listen to your thoughts with empathy and curiosity and reflect on them in writing. Practiced regularly, this simple yet powerfully effective method gradually opens a path to self-trust. Other frequently reported benefits include: deepened powers of attention, increased self-confidence, greater intimacy and spontaneity in relationships, enhanced emotional health, and awakened spirituality."

We spent the remainder of our time together that evening avoiding the usual gut-wrenching self-exploration we normally do in our proprioceptive "writes" by instead gabbing away like magpies while discussing the whole concept of hipness. We provided analyses of such questions as what, if anything, the difference is between "hip" and "hipster," whether there's an inherent aloofness to hip people, what the levels and categories of hipness are, and what qualities a hip person possesses as opposed to a "hip mama." Lynne demonstrated an encyclopedic amount of knowledge on the subject, and though nailing down a precise definition proved to be impossible, she composed a verbal dissertation that clarified the thesis I had been chewing on since my Material Objects experience: Any hipness that I myself may have possessed had evaporated the moment Craig's winning sperm penetrated the outer layer of my ovum, way back in February 1997. Furthermore, it also became clear that the closer I got to the age of forty, the larger the abyss grew between me and hipness.

And then I remembered that years ago, when I was a young and impressionable lass in my early twenties, my worldly and writerly friend Stona Fitch had commented on the attire of some lame-ass poser and quipped: "A leather jacket does not a cool man make."

WRITING GROUP

DON'T FEEL SO BAD! ONE TIME I TOOK A FUTON OVER TO CATHOLIC CHARITIES TO DONATE IT TO THE REFUGEE RESETTLEMENT PROGRAM — YOU KNOW, WHERE THEY GIVE FURNITURE TO FAMILIES WHO JUST GOT HERE AND DON'T HAVE ANY FURNITURE. JOHN AND I HAD GOTTEN THE FUTON WHEN WE LIVED TOGETHER IN BOSTON — IT WAS A DELUXE MODEL: NOT TOP OF THE LINE BUT NOT A PIECE OF CRAP, EITHER — AND THE MATTRESS WAS A LITTLE LUMPY, BUT NOT TOO BAD, AND THE FRAME WAS MISSING A SLAT BECAUSE NAOMI JUMPED ON IT ONCE AND BROKE IT - BUT REALLY, IT LOOKED PRETTY GOOD. ANYWAYS, I DROVE IT OVER TO CATHOLIC CHARITIES AND THEY WOULDN'T TAKE IT! EVEN THE PRISONERS WHO WERE WORKING THERE IN THEIR BLUE WORK SUITS — LOADING AND UNLOADING THE DONATIONS AT THE DROP-OFF CENTER — EVEN THE PRISONERS FELT SORRY FOR ME AS THEY LOADED MY FUTON BACK INTO THE CAR. I FELT LIKE SUCH A LOSER THAT I DIDN'T EVEN THINK I DESERVED A CUP OF COFFEE AT THAT HIP CAFE WHERE THEY MAKE DESIGNS IN THE FOAM OF YOUR LATTE.

HIP NEW HAIRCUT

LYNNE

RAYE

DELIA

This phrase became especially resonant as I began to take stock of my own tragic unhipness. I searched for any outward signs of hipness, which Lynne had delineated in her verbal dissertation. The following addendum is entitled "Physical Signs of Hipness Which I Possess, But Only in an Unhip Way."

One: Multiple piercings do not a hip mama make.

The nose. The lip. The belly button. The nipple. The tongue. The labia. All hip locales for piercings. I don't have piercings in those places. My piercings are all on my earlobes. But ear piercings are only hip these days when the ear hole is stretched successively larger and larger, until it is the size of a half-dollar. This process is called gauging.

Me, I have four tiny holes in both my right and left earlobes which were a result of teenage zealotry and easy access to ice cubes and needles. My parents had forbidden me to get my ears pierced for so many years that when I was finally allowed to get a tiny pair of gold studs punctured into my lobes at the age of thirteen, the process unleashed all the pent-up desire for ear piercing I'd held inside since the age of six. I went berserk and spent many a Saturday night locked in our tiny second-floor bathroom with the slanted ceiling, jabbing my ears silly and also the ears of those friends of mine I could rope into spending a night over at my piercing emporium. At that time, it was kinda cool to sport multiple ear holes, adorned with a cute assortment of studs and hoops, a constellation that looked particularly fetching when worn in combination with Jennifer-Beals-in-*Flashdance*–style sweatshirts, the necks of which had been cut off to expose a bit of pubescent shoulder and training bra.

Anyhoo, the tragedy inherent in this tale is that, after all of that waiting and begging and hoping for pierced ears, after convincing myself that my life would finally be perfect once I got pierced ears, and then after all the holes I managed to jab into my noggin, after all of that, my piercings presently lie unadorned and quite possibly defunct, since the holes have sat empty for so long. I don't even have it in me to scrounge around in my dusty jewelry box to come up with a pair of studs. I guess I got out of the habit of wearing anything that could be torn through my flesh when George was six or so months old and liked to reach up and grab my earrings while he was nursing and give 'em a good ol' yank.

There was a brief time, however, when I entertained the idea of getting a belly-button piercing. All the hip women at the beach seemed to be sporting them. But once I did some careful consideration of the subject and projected out in time, imagining what my body was bound to look like in, say, a decade or thereabouts, I quickly shut that idea out of my mind.

I have come to terms with my unhip piercings. They are, after all, tiny holes in my earlobes—barely visible to the naked eye. The same case cannot be made, however, for the permanent blue ink and scarification I suffered at the hands of a geriatric tattoo artist, which brings me to my second point.

Two: Tattoos do not a hip mama make.

It seems to me that tattooing technology and skill have improved a thousandfold since I got my tatt—almost twenty years ago. The colors seem brighter and less prone to fading, the outlines seem crisper, the designs more artful, and the work itself . . . Let's just say that it must be nice to be able to walk around without having to answer the question, "What is your tattoo of?" whenever you wear a tank top.

Not that I have regrets. Well, okay, I have a few. I guess in retrospect I should have done a little research to determine the caliber of skill that the "artist" I chose to drill a vibrating needle into my shoulder whilst injecting permanent ink into the wound might have possessed.

Ah, youth! I was but a lass of twenty-two and was so excited to get the tatt that I overlooked one niggling detail. I was so caught up in the design that I wanted (the Little Prince, from the French novella of the same name) that I neglected to use deductive analytical skills and conclude that there must be a *reason* no one was standing at the booth of the octogenarian with jailhouse tatts running up and down his grizzled arms.

I must say, though, that my tattoo has provided hours of entertainment in bars and other fine establishments when drunkards approach me and use the line "I like your tattoo. What is it?" and I merely reply, "What do *you* think it is?"

Three: A spiky haircut does not a hip mama make.

Back in my mid-thirties, I flirted with the idea of trying to achieve the kind of hairstyle I'd seen some really hip-looking mamas wearing: short and spiky—one would almost say slightly tousled, urban street-urchinish, chic yet devil-may-care—and created with the help of a really good stylist and some expensive hair product, slathered onto the fingertips and then sculpted into the coiffure. I'd actually had a celebrity encounter with this do back in the early nineties—*way* B.C.—when Craig and I were at a party in the Jamaica Plain neighborhood of Boston and I looked up from my alcohol-induced trance to see Aimee Mann[12] standing in the doorway. Tall, self-assured, and freakin' gorgeous, Aimee walked by the beanbag chair in which I was slumped, and as I caught a whiff of rawhide from the jacket she was wearing, I thought, *Someday I will wear my hair like that. Someday, I will be that hip!*

12. Who recorded the album *Voices Carry* with her band 'Til Tuesday in the eighties and then went on to make it big as a very hip solo artist.

MY HAIRCUT...

WAS SUPPOSED TO LOOK LIKE THIS

AIMEE MANN

1/4" STUBBLE DYED PLATINUM BLONDE

I AM SO BAD ASS!

fondle

DELUSIONAL FRAU

DAD

YOU SHOULD LET YOUR HAIR GROW OUT TO BE ... GOOD LOOKING—LIKE IT USED TO BE.

HER LOOKS ARE REALLY STARTING TO GO DOWNHILL.

WOULD YOU LIKE SOME CANTALOUPE?

MOM

Over the years, my vision morphed. Perhaps the ego-shredding vulnerability I experienced while pushing babies out of my vagina had scared the crap out of me. I don't know. But after Dora was born I decided I wanted to create a look for myself that said, *Yes, I am nursing a toddler, but I do believe that I could kick your ass.* Ultimately, this fantasy involved a shiny black latex body stocking and high-heeled boots à la Trinity in *The Matrix*.[13]

However, in order to look good in that kind of a getup, I'd have to spend months lifting weights and getting full cardio benefits. What I could change quickly was my hair. And the opportunity to do so presented itself during our lice abatement (see pages 69–76). After Craig shaved my head, I dyed the quarter-inch stubble platinum blonde, thinking that the color would enhance my badass look. However, my family began sending me carefully worded verbal cues that pointed to the ugly truth: I looked a lot less like Aimee Mann or Trinity and a whole heckuva lot more like late-eighties fitness guru Susan Powter after a particularly grotesque binge involving Captain-Morgan-and-Cokes and fried dough.

I ask you: How unhip is that?

Thirteen: The Strange Case of Dr. M

was another Shabbat at Jake and

Leah's house. The kids whipped themselves up into a frenzy playing with oobleck[1] at the counter, while the adults gabbed and dined on Leah's delicious grilled chicken and white bean salad, which I openly marveled that she'd had the fortitude to prepare, seeing as her hubby Jake was out of town for the second consecutive weekend and she'd been awake for, like, three days delivering babies.

Just as the conversation was getting really good 'n' lubed by the vino, the children all started melting down, and Jesse and Betsy exited quickly with their green-food-coloring-stained kinder (Nina and Miles), Delia pulled Abby and Gus out of the mix, Craig split to go get George from baseball practice, Leah went upstairs to start putting Raizel and Oscar to bed, and it was just me and Dora and Dr. M left there, on the couch.[2]

---

1. Based on the fictional gooey green precipitation in Dr. Seuss's book *Bartholomew and the Oobleck,* this not-really-liquid, not-really-solid mixture fascinates kids of all ages and will keep them occupied for a really long time. The best part is that oobleck is oh-so easy to prepare: Mix together two cups of cornstarch, three drops of green food coloring, and enough water to make a thick mixture in a large container with a flat bottom. Let the kids go wild.

2. Dr. M's hubby had taken their child, Sam, to his parents' for the evening.

Because Dora had managed to take a three-hour nap that afternoon, something she hadn't done since she was a newborn, she was totally amped to party, and so she laughed maniacally when I mentioned heading home to bed. She jumped up and down on the futon and nearly kicked Dr. M's drink over, and when Leah came down to fetch a stuffed animal (I do believe it was a Webkin) for her daughter Raizel, she suggested that Dora and I sleep over. I was as psyched about it as Dora, since I, too, love sleepover action (and what girl in her right mind wouldn't, after all?) and because I'd consumed more than my fair share of wine and wanted to settle in and gab the night away rather than get behind the wheel of my Subaru with a shrieking daughter in tow.

I took Dora upstairs, where she snuggled into Raizel's bed while Leah read aloud from a book about a giraffe who comes to realize that his differences (long neck, spots) from other animals make him special—or something like that. To be honest, I wasn't really paying attention. I was pretty blissed out there on the cozy foldaway bed on which I was lying.

Leah finished the giraffe book and went downstairs, and I stayed for a while, eavesdropping on the girls' discussion of the pros and cons of snowsuits and what they should name Raizel's Webkinz®, and I was lulled nearly to sleep by their sweetness and purity.

Eventually, I was able to pull myself up to an erect position and kiss the girls goodnight, and I headed downstairs into a den of depravity, where the big girls were already laughing and sharing stories with more, shall we say, "adult" themes. I jumped right in and told them about the link that our friend Lynne had e-mailed me that day of a video snippet of Colin Farrell bonking a *Playboy* centerfold named Nicole Something-or-Other,[3] and so we sparked up the iMac and googled "Colin Farrell sex video." Wham!—there we were, huddled around Leah's computer but more like transported via the World Wide Web to some tawdry locale, where we witnessed a very well-endowed Mr. Farrell servicing his moaning companion, who had shaved her pubic hair into the shape of a triangle, so that at first I was confused and thought her pubes were a goatee on someone else's face until my depraved companions set me straight.

Because it was less than a minute long, the Colin Farrell sequence[4] held us stupefied, and we played it over and over again—right-clicking the mouse to start it rolling again and enlarging the image on the screen so that Colin Farrell's face took on a pixelated and supersmutty quality—until we heard the tiny footfall on the stairs that signaled that one of the kinder from the realm of innocence was descending into our realm of filth. And so, quick as a mouse can click, I exited the porn site and whirled around just in time to see my daughter standing there and to field her excellent question.

3. Not to be confused with Nicole Chaison, aka the Hausfrau—although the similarities are striking.

4. I later learned that the sequence we watched was culled from a fifteen-minute extravaganza, which you could purchase on the Internet and which prompted Colin Farrell to sue his ex-playmate; both versions have since been removed from the Internet. I've tried many times—many, many times—since then to find the sequence we watched that night, and it is just plain *gone*.

I tossed off some casual explanation about looking for something on the computer and then scooped up my little girl and carried her back upstairs, where her friend Raizel was already sound asleep. So as not to disturb a sleeping child, I took Dora into the guest room. We crawled into the large and supercomfortable bed there, and I read her several books and sang her a song and gave her a back rub, but nothing helped to lull her to sleep. Finally, after a good half hour or so, she complained of thirst, and I went in search of a cup but couldn't find one anywhere in the realm of innocence. I told Dora to stay put while I fetched a cup from downstairs and brought the water up to her—but she would have none of it.

She threw her head back and wailed, and I think what really got to me were her teeth—or the dwindling number of them, actually, as she'd lost both the top and bottom front teeth over the past few months, which had rendered her mouth incredibly vulnerable looking, with tender sockets exposing the spaces where her teeth once had been. Dora really loved her teeth—especially the top ones, which had grown in somewhat misshapen when she was but a teething babe and which we called her "wuzzly" teeth, because they did, in fact, look wuzzly.

5. And, really, who does?

In addition, I felt guilty because I had actually been the one who had pulled out her last wuzzly tooth. It had been hanging by a thread and driving Dora crazy for several days, and after a long and involved psychological struggle in our downstairs bathroom, during which she sat on the sink and implored me to pop the tooth out for her, she then screamed bloody murder when I did so, castigating me for having followed her orders.

I'd even tried to make it up to her by helping her craft a letter to the tooth fairy, explaining why Dora should both a) be able to keep her wuzzly teeth forever, secured inside her "Somewhere Over the Rainbow" jewelry box; and b) still receive tooth-fairy booty[6] under her pillow the following morning.

But I can tell that she blames me for her wuzzly-tooth loss, and I guess I have to chalk it up to the intricacies of the mother/daughter struggle.

Anyhoo, long story short: I caved in and let Dora accompany me on my journey into the maw of depravity, down the stairs in search of a cup to fill with life-sustaining water.

---

6. A big, golden Sacagawea dollar and a faux pearl necklace.

As we neared the bottom of the stairwell, I began to hear what sounded like the moanings and gruntings and sloppy sounds of the Colin Farrell video, but I didn't trust my own ears, reasoning that there could be no way that my pals would *still* be watching the porno, as it had been at least a half an hour since I'd gone away to the realm of innocence. But sho' nuff: As my daughter and I made our way through the hall, past the dining room, and into the kitchen/family-room area, where Leah and Jake house their computer—separated from us by only a stand of cubbies—the unmistakable sounds of porn wafted throughout, and it became clear that my cohorts were indeed still glued to the screen.

In a panic, I shouted out several warnings and tried to pull Dora back, but she scrambled ahead, with me after her. As we rounded the cubbies and entered the computer area, I was both amused and relieved to see Dr. M on her knees on the floor, yanking the computer cord from its socket, sweat droplets glistening upon her brow from her laborious attempt to shield my child from the sight of Colin Farrell's you-know-what.

And if that is not true heroism, then I don't know what is.

Fourteen: Our Journey to the Center of the (Happiest Celebration on) Earth™

Craig's father, Chuck, turned seventy and decided that, rather than throw himself a big party, he'd fly the whole family down for four days of sun and fun at a certain theme park in central Florida, which—on the eerie DVD that arrived at our house along with our itineraries—was currently undertaking "the Happiest Celebration on Earth."

As a Yankee, it's my God-given duty to be suspicious of any activity south of the Mason-Dixon line, and the prospect of going "down there" in the winter stirred up all sorts of muck and unleashed the ghost of my Puritan Forefather, who spoke through me, as if I were a medium at a séance.

But, of course, my children would have none of it. They met my caustic tirade with the quizzical-yet-disappointed innocence that never fails to shut me up and make me feel like the monster I am. So I decided to shut my big yapper and suck it up—for the kids' sake and also for Chuck, whose birthday it was and who was shelling out the big bucks for the trip. I put on my happy face and grabbed my journal and chronicled our journey of four days, down, down, down into the center of the Happiest Celebration on Earth!™

But before we could get there, we had to pass through other worlds and overcome the many challenges we encountered. The first one was Trying-to-Get-to-the-Bus-Station World.

---

1. Remember that our trip to Puerto Rico, chronicled on pages 107–109, was also generously funded by my father-in-law.

Craig and I had planned to wake the kids up at 4:00 a.m. and leave the house at 4:30 so that we could drive the two miles to the bus station, where we'd ditch our car, buy our tickets, and board a southbound bus scheduled to leave for Boston's Logan Airport at 5:00 a.m. Catching that bus was critical, as it would allow us just enough time to then make our 8:30 a.m. flight. However, at 4:50 a.m., we exploded out of the house, coats and scarves and gloves a-flapping, and found ourselves in the first snowstorm of the season, a nor'easter, which had taken us quite by surprise. Craig and I had been under the (apparently mistaken) impression that global warming had already so significantly altered the weather patterns as to obviate the need for ice scrapers and snow shovels and salt and sand, and the ghost of my Puritan Forefather chastised me yet again as I desperately tried to scrape a quarter inch of ice off the windshield of our Subaru with the broken half of a clear plastic CD case, while the kids frolicked in the snow and Craig disappeared into the basement in search of last year's scrapers. Four inches of fluffy snow masked the quarter inch of ice which lay darkly beneath, causing the driveway to become cartoonishly slippery, an occasion George seized upon to perform his "I-can't-get-up-the-driveway-and-into-the-car-because-I-keep-slipping-down" routine.

The scene culminated in my complete loss of control after the CD case snapped and splintered in my hand, sending shards of plastic flying through the predawn snowflakes.

I screamed like a wretch at Craig, whom I blamed for our predicament, just like I always do in times of crisis.

Anyhoo, the real miracle of the Christmas season was that we somehow managed to make it to the bus station, park the car, buy the tickets, board the bus, stow our stuff, and secure headphones, so that the kids could watch that movie *Cars* on the dangling video screens—all before 5:00 a.m., when the bus pulled away from the curb and roared toward warmer climes and happier celebrations. I even took the opportunity to apologize to Craig for my horrendous behavior back in the driveway while he and I snuggled in the way-back, near the bathroom, steaming up the windows as we went.

We made it to Logan on time, and the second leg of our journey was a flight from Boston to New York on a puddle jumper in extremely high winds. The stronger-stomached half of our foursome sat behind me and George, and the plane lurched and bobbed and dipped like a near-dead mouse being batted about by a gigantic cosmic kitty cat. It was an occasion for me to practice my skills at calming my child while suffering deeply myself. I held a barf bag for him and rubbed his back and whispered soothing words while I kept myself from projectile vomiting when our plane took a nosedive, believing we'd all end up a twisted and smoking pile of charred metal and flesh and bones in someone's back-yard on Long Island (the potential upside being that I'd finally get to visit the Hamptons).

Once we landed at LaGuardia, I was so flipping happy to be alive that I didn't even reprimand George when he smooshed his face against the Plexiglas barricade at the security checkpoint, although I murmured a warning to him about the germs of millions of travelers smeared upon it. Craig and I were scolded, however, for failing to encase Dora's special sunscreen[2] in a plastic ziplock baggie, as is now standard procedure when traveling with creams and gels as per the Department of Homeland Security. Furthermore, Dora's unbelievably expensive Odwalla orange juice (which we had broken down and purchased for her amid her shrieks of thirst) was confiscated by security because she'd failed to guzzle it down before entering the checkpoint. Luckily, security failed to detect the bomb[3] George had cleverly concealed in his rectal cavity.

We arrived safely in Orlando after a smooth and uneventful flight from LaGuardia, and after we'd had a chance to check in and change into our shorts and T-shirts and run around a little, the whole family convened for dinner in the dining area of the Contemporary, our hotel, which boasted a monorail stop inside the lobby.

2. The one that *doesn't* give her a really bad rash all over her body.

3. A *stink bomb,* that is, of nearly lethal caliber, which George let fly en route to Orlando, at 30,000 feet.

4. As in, spermicidal jams and jellies.

I shared several glasses of wine with my sister-in-law, Elisa, as we gossiped about what had happened since the last time we'd seen each other, while the children sat, silent and still, under the behemoth cathode-ray-tube altar watching old Walt Disney cartoons, like the one where Mickey Mouse fights a fire with a pair of scissors and cuts the fire in half. I was struck by how masterful and great those old cartoons were. So funny! So inventive! The children were enthralled!

I began to wonder, then, how we got from there to here.

My father-in-law paced nervously as he waited for the red light to flash on the handheld device he'd been given, which would summon us to our awaiting table. When the light finally flashed, we assembled in the dining area, adjacent to Chef Mickey's—a special restaurant where the characters walk around and come over to your table and hug you and your children and pose for photographs and videos and sign autographs with their furry, oversize hands.

Apparently, you have to have reservations at Chef Mickey's in order to interact with the characters—a fact lost on me, especially because the only thing separating Chef Mickey's from our table was a giant potted fern, which I climbed over with Dora, because she had been jumping up and down and pointing at the characters and yelling their names as they paraded by. I became confused and then enraged when Dora squealed with delight and ran over to meet Mickey, Minnie, Goofy, Pluto, and Donald and they all completely ignored her and hammed it up with the other children and families seated at Chef Mickey's. Once Craig explained it to me, it all made sense (sort of), but I found it impossible to explain to my five-year-old daughter, whose tears were like daggers in my heart.

And as if that wasn't enough damage, the next morning we set out for Disney's Hollywood Studios. George roped as many of us as he could into his master plan, which involved a ride called the Tower of Terror, and I meanwhile opted to take Dora over to Ariel's Grotto—billed as a "musical celebration of the magic of the Little Mermaid"—where we waited in line for forty-five minutes to enter and then, of course, were *amply* rewarded for our patience.

For those unfamiliar with Disney's movie franchise of the classic Hans Christian Andersen tale, the plot goes like this: Ariel, the youngest mermaid daughter of King Triton, ignores her dad's admonitions and explores the surface of the ocean, where she encounters Eric—a Ken-dollish prince—whom she saves when a storm capsizes his ship. Ariel resuscitates Prince Eric by singing to him and then, of course, falls in love with him. Ariel longs to live in Eric's world, so she visits Ursula, a sea witch, who agrees to turn Ariel into a human under one condition: She must sacrifice her voice—forever. Ariel goes for it. Yikes!

I squirmed in horror and Dora sat at rapt attention as we watched the Barbie-like actress playing Ariel give away her voice to the loud, bossy, and wicked Ursula, who looked like Divine and sounded like Harvey Fierstein and had the best lines by far. It could have all made for some hilarious camp—if only! After it was all over, we exited the amphitheater and were immediately corralled inside a Disney store that sold (guess what?) Ariel bathing suits and dolls and posters and crowns and costumes and fairy wands and high-heeled princess shoes. Luckily, Dora did not fall for it (thank you, parenting gods!) and seemed to want to get out of there as badly as I did. We snuggled together on a bench outside while I recouped from Ariel's Grotto, but I was badly shaken.

Luckily, George and Craig found us soon thereafter and distracted us by providing a blow-by-blow account of their visit to the Tower of Terror. And then it was on to other rides and shows and other worlds.

The warm sun. The aquamarine pool. The chaise longue. The poolside bar that offered alcoholic beverages I could charge to our "meal plan." My journal. The Jonathan Franzen memoir I was in the middle of, which made me belly-laugh (a rarity). Free babysitting, during which the kids could frolic in the pool and color pictures of Disney characters. We left this world behind in pursuit of a larger, louder, brighter, and more garish world.

I speak, of course, of the Magic Kingdom®.

The next morning we set out bright and early on a steamboat[5] to the dazzling gates that open upon the Kingdom.[6] George and his cousins and the other adults headed over to the Tomorrowland® Indy Speedway, while Dora and I waited in line for over an hour before boarding the two-minute flight atop the Dumbo ride. We then searched for the Disney princesses, whom Dora had had her heart set on meeting ever since she first saw them in the eerie DVD that was sent to our house along with our itinerary.

5. To get to the Magic Kingdom Theme Park, which we could see from our hotel, we could travel by boat, taxi, monorail, or bus. It was impossible, however, to walk there.

6. Which could also be called "Cardiac-Defibrillator World."

Chuck caught up with us and offered to watch Dora while I visited Ladies'-Bathroom World. When I returned, he informed me that Craig had taken all the kids into The Haunted Mansion, a ride in which hologram ghosts pop out at you as your cart travels along a track inside a pitch-black haunted house. Long story short: Dora and George are now unable to be alone for any length of time in any room of our house, especially at nighttime, which makes for some interesting sleeping arrangements. Dora wakes several times a night and flails about in the throes of nightmarish visions of hologram ghosts popping out at her. This must have been what they meant on that DVD when they said, "At Disney, you'll make memories that will last a lifetime."

Lest you think me a complete curmudgeon, I must confess to the highlight of our trip, which was finally getting to go on Space Mountain with George. It was an absolute thrill to zoom through the dark rollercoaster ride, lit only by twinkling stars, and to hold hands with my boy while we screamed with delight. Plus, I think the ghost of my Puritan Forefather must have had a massive coronary on the ride, because his pinched and anus-like face didn't pop up again for the rest of our journey.

And speaking of journeys, my favorite world of all the ones we passed through was the one we entered when our Concord Trailways bus from Logan Airport crossed over the Piscataquis River Bridge, past the white gas tank with the big red lobster painted on it, and past the sign that says "Welcome to Maine: The Way Life Should Be."

Just like Dorothy in *The Wizard of Oz,* the whole time we were partaking of the Happiest Celebration on Earth™, all I really wanted to do was go home. I have a much better time hanging around with Craig and the kids and our friends right here, in our very own living room.

The Hausfrauian Tales

Regrettable Parenting Moments Galore!

One night, I was visited—as if in a dream—by Chaucer,
who took me by the hand and flung me up on the back
of his white horse and took me on a pilgrimage.
From every shires ende of Engeland to Canterbury we
wende, stopping here and there along the way at taverns
and sharing flagons of fermented spirits and lots of laughs.
I regaled him with tales of motherhood and regrettable
parenting moments galore.

One: The Tale of How It Came to Be that My Toddler Gave Herself a Bath in the Sink

was compelled to write. I'd been itching to write all day—I woke up that way.

Mind you, it had been a fine day, a full day. I had been with the kids for eleven hours, and I was really looking forward to some time to myself after dinner so that I could squirrel myself away and fulfill my urges in my journal. During the meal, however, Craig reminded me that, right after dinner, he would have to go back out to a meeting that would last several hours.

I just couldn't push the muses off any longer, so I did what any self-respecting hausfrau would do in that situation: I let my children go feral whilst I wrote. Because we don't do playpens and because two-year-old Dora was excited about engaging in water-play, I set her up in the bathroom, just feet from my writing desk, with a sink full of tepid water, some cups and spoons, and a step stool on which to stand. George was caught up in playing Egyptian pharaoh warrior and would check in with me every few minutes to receive his orders from on high.

Time passed. I got really sucked into the writing— I wrote and wrote and entered that most excellent place that is rare for me, hard to describe but similar to really good sex in that everything else just drops away. I was on fire, baby! The muses—and the pages of my journal—were much satisfied.

At some point, I became vaguely aware that Dora had been repeatedly entering the room and placing articles of her clothing on my desk. I didn't, however, hear or see her drag the tall stool (one of a set of four

that we all sit on at meals around the kitchen "peninsula") into the bathroom. This fact deeply concerns me, as she would have had to drag the clunky wooden stool right past me at my desk—and the damn thing is heavy.

I was still writing away furiously when George came in and gave me a Mama-must-be-writing-style hug, which involves placing his hands around my neck and then hanging off the back of my chair, thus nearly asphyxiating me. It was at this moment that Dora started calling out for me. She didn't sound distressed in the slightest, so I sent George to investigate. His frenzied cry shot me right out of my seat and into the bathroom, where I encountered my naked toddler lounging in the sink basin.

Later on, when Craig came home from his meeting, I told him about the evening and its similarities to Grammy Mil's experience sixty years before (chronicled on page 33). It was hard to process the incident because, like with so many parenting issues, I felt so many conflicting emotions simultaneously.[1]

Craig didn't see the incident in a negative light. He thought it illuminated Dora's resourcefulness, and he focused on the fact that no harm was done. For me, however, the experience opened up new and unforeseen vistas of parental angst: What if I, like my grandmother before me, had failed to hear Dora calling out to me and George hadn't been there to check on her? What if she'd slipped and cracked her head open while I sat there, writing away?

Two: The Tale of How It Came to Be that I Urinated into a Tupperware Container

I'M A 36-YEAR-OLD WOM-AN WHO CAN'T STAND UP.

BEFORE THE MEDICATION

LOOKIN' GOOD!

MUSCLE RELAXER

AFTER THE MEDICATION

OKAY. SO, YEAH.... I WANNA GO SIDDOWN.

slosh

THE GALA EVENT

VINO DÉ RICK

I'd thrown my back out hauling laundry and Dora down three flights of stairs to the basement washer and dryer. My friend the physician's assistant—who shall remain nameless—generously prescribed me some muscle relaxers I could take while nursing. They did the trick of masking my symptoms, allowing me to function (i.e., I could almost stand erect) and continue to carry out my hausfrau duties. I was grateful, since we were busy preparing for Craig's big fund-raiser for Cultivating Community that night, a rah-sha-sha affair in which a talented local artist was donating a percentage of the money from the sale of his paintings to Craig's organization.

I liberally dosed myself with the medication and got gussied up, and we set off for the fund-raiser. I drank a few glasses of wine while hobnobbing with the artsy, well-heeled guests and soon found it challenging to construct coherent sentences. I kept trying to explain my condition but made things worse by attempting to converse.

That evening of booze and pills really cost me. I awoke the next morning in such excruciating pain that George had to help me out of bed. I vowed to change my ways and made an appointment with a chiropractor. But since I had to have a bunch of diagnostic tests before she would adjust my train wreck of a spine, I had no choice but to press on with the day.

To further complicate matters, we'd had our toilet removed from the downstairs bathroom the week before, and the only functional toilet was on the third

floor of the house. We'd planned to install a new toilet, washer, and dryer downstairs, but we hadn't gotten around to it yet.

That morning, I stood in our kitchen, having a racking back spasm, when the urge to urinate struck. There was no way in hell I could make it up the steep steps to the third floor to use the toilet. So what did I do? I solved this hausfrau dilemma as follows: I grabbed an empty Tupperware container, peed in it, and dumped the contents into the sink, while my children looked on, wide-eyed and slack-jawed. I then rinsed the container out and placed it in the dishwasher and explained to my children that they should never imitate nor reveal what they had witnessed me doing. It was a learning moment for all involved!

Three: The Tale of How It Came to Be that I Cleaned Maggots Out from Under the Cover of a Car Seat

ne early autumn, the foul odor in our Subaru Forester became intolerable. The stench (complex and hard to describe, but with definite hints of spoiled dairy products and fermented fruit, blended with undercurrents of mold and miscellaneous decaying organic matter) had been increasing in intensity since the second week in August.

The only way we could drive home from the Common Ground Fair was to roll down all four windows and stick our heads out, taking huge gulps of air, whenever we came to stoplights.

We needed to act.

Craig and I searched the car from glove compartment to spare tire several times when the odor first struck our nostrils back in August. We looked for a forgotten diaper, a decaying rodent, or festering seashore spoils like starfish. No luck. We removed a few apple cores, wedged behind the kids' car seats, as well as a sippy cup with contents so putrid that we tossed it in the nearest garbage can rather than risk opening and transferring it to the dishwasher. As we progressed into Indian summer, the smell just kept getting worse.

Determined to find its source, I finally removed the cloth covering from Dora's car seat. There, lodged deep within the Britax's plastic frame, was the mother lode of putrescence.

Consumers, take note! The Britax contains a serious design flaw: a four-inch-deep well on each side of the seat, right under the armrests. An innovative toddler can easily pull up the cover and deposit quite an assortment of food and nonfood items in these wells. Just like mine did.

After Dora's tampering, the Britax wells had become home to the most ungodly assortment of rotten matter I've ever witnessed. The right repository contained all manner of nastiness: moldy fruit, some sort of fungus, and chunks of unidentifiable brown stuff. The left repository contained even more grotesque decay than the right, and was topped off with a slew of maggots and, interestingly, the ear of Mr. Potato Head, which we'd given up for lost.

I'm not at all sure how the maggots entered the picture, but let me tell you this: They sure made for an afternoon replete with gagging whilst we cleaned and disinfected!

Four: The Tale of Billy Elliot

STACK OF BOOKS

OPERATING INSTRU...
THE BIG RUMPUS
SIBLINGS WITHOUT RIVALRY
THE FAMILY BED
HOW TO TALK SO KIDS WILL LISTEN AND
LISTEN SO KIDS WILL TALK
YOUR SPIRITED CHILD
PLAYFUL PARENTING
THE OUT-OF-SYNC CHILD 1
WHY CAN'T MY CHILD BEHAVE?
YOUR SIX-YEAR-OLD
YOUR TWO-YEAR-O...

ON MY BEDSIDE TABLE

MY RECOLLEC-
TION OF
THE FILM
BILLY
ELLIOT

y obsessive attention to my children's emotional and physical needs probably qualifies me for inclusion as a case study in the *Big Book of Psychological Disorders*. I've read every book on childrearing, mothering, and "spirited" children—but I'm still just a mixed-up jumble of nerves who functions primarily thanks to coffee (the a.m. tonic) and wine (the p.m. tonic).

As our children grow, my hubby and I find it increasingly difficult to make consistently sound parenting choices. Take, for example, the case of *Billy Elliot*.

When George was six, he started asking questions about dance. He wanted to know what kinds of dance there were and what it was like to be a boy who dances. My mind clicked back to the movie *Billy Elliot*, a wonderful film Craig and I had seen in the theater four years earlier, when it had just been released.[2] Craig and I both loved the film. We remembered it as the sweet, lighthearted journey of a young boy (Billy) who taps and pliés his way out of crushing poverty in Northern England and into our hearts.

I thought *Billy Elliot* would be the perfect movie for George—him being a boy and being interested in dancing—and so we drove over to Videoport and rented it for home viewing.

---

1. I'd like to write a book called *The Out-of-Sync Mother*.

2. Since the kids were born, Craig and I have gotten to see one or two movies a year in the theater. You'd think we could retain the basic gist of the films.

I'm not sure why I didn't stop to check the rating on the back of the movie box; perhaps I was so confident in my memory of the endearing film that checking the rating never occurred to me. In any case, we came home, made some popcorn, and the four of us settled in on the couch to watch *Billy Elliot*.

About twenty minutes into the film, during a scene depicting Billy's foul-mouthed father berating his son for wanting to dance, I became increasingly uncomfortable and then watched in horror as Billy's brother was brutally beaten by police for striking at the coal mine where he worked.

Both Craig and I were aghast at the gaping disparity between what we remembered of the film and what we were actually seeing on the screen. I guess the presence of children changes one's experience of the medium.

I checked the back of the movie box, and indeed, it was rated R—for language and violence. Whoops!

George posed some tough questions, which stymied me. And though I did my best to explain the situation in terms he could understand, I was filled with remorse as I thought back to my own childhood and to my first movie, which my dad took me to see when I was six.

It was called *The Bluebird,* and I still remember it to this day. It haunts me that my children were exposed to their first R-rated movie at the ages of six and two. For Chrissakes! I was in *college* when I saw my first R-rated movie. It was *Last Tango in Paris*—and I don't really remember much about the film, except that there was scant dialogue and Marlon Brando kept his pants on when he had sex with a woman much younger than himself.

But don't think for a moment that my poor parenting would go unpunished, or that my overwhelming feelings of guilt and shame would be enough of a consequence for the Hausfrau.

Oh, no! The parenting gods saw to it that I was really reamed: George's speech was peppered with the f-word for the next several weeks, causing me to wince at each utterance, and, of course, spurring his sister to mimic him, which was even worse.

But as in so many other instances in which I've royally screwed up and have feared that my children would be irreparably damaged, George all of a sudden seemed to get over the whole *Billy Elliot* debacle and moved on of his own accord. He magically stopped using the f-word altogether, and I've never heard him say it again.

3. Or was it rated X?

Five: The Tale of Republican Man

took the kids with me to the polls on Tuesday, November 2, 2004, feeling full of hope—for the country, for democracy, for my children (who were currently running feral in the basement of the Woodfords Congregational Church and regaling voters and pollsters with some hard-hitting questions and good old-fashioned high jinks)—for the first time in four years. I was primed to cast my vote against Him-Who-Shall-Not-Be-Named, and when I stepped into the voting booth and pulled the blue-and-white-striped curtain closed behind me, and then as I filled in the little bubble next to John Kerry's name, my eyes welled up with tears and my writing hand shook with excitement. We'd all been through so much, hadn't we?

And so, that night, late into the wee hours, as my hubby and I watched the U.S. map on the TV screen filling up with more and more and more red, I was incredulous. How could it be? How could it be? I finally went to bed, unsure of what the morning would bring—but none too hopeful.

Cut to the next morning. I came downstairs, and as I rounded the corner and entered the kitchen, I glanced nervously at my bleary-eyed hubby and our eldest child, who blurted out the stomach-wrenching news and who seemed to revel in the fact that I—Great Mother and Knower-of-All-Things-in-the-Universe—had been dead wrong in my prediction about the outcome of the 2004 election.

It was a steep downhill journey after that, too, I can tell you, culminating in the car ride to the grocery store later that afternoon during which I openly wept while listening to Kerry's concession speech, which was partially drowned out by the concerned queries of my kinder. I was just plain heartbroken, and I couldn't friggin' get over it.

Our house went into communication lockdown for at least a week: no newspapers, no TV, no phone. I couldn't bring myself to read the e-mails that were piling up in my inbox—even the ones from celebs like Michael Moore, with subject headings like "10 Reasons Not to Slit Your Wrists After the Election." The point was, I didn't *want* to be cheered up. I was pissed off and disgusted and—from a global viewpoint—embarrassed as all get-out. Whoops! Sorry, world!

Unlike Eckhart Tolle, I was having a great deal of trouble seeing the oneness that I share with my Republican brethren or the perfection of the world or much of anything besides the big stinkin' mess occupying the White House. And I couldn't decide which was the worst-case scenario: a) the possibility that there had been a massive Republican conspiracy to rig voting machines and steal the election; or b) the possibility that 51 percent of Americans actually voted for Him-Who-Shall-Not-Be-Named.

I wanted to wallow in my misery! And wallow I did.

The following week, though still wallowing, I had enough wherewithal to take George to his martial arts class. There's this father there . . . oh, let's just call him Republican Man. His son started taking lessons around the same time George did. Republican Man always pulls up in the parking lot in his behemoth automobile bedecked with bumper stickers of the sort that offend every cell in my body. Though I loathe everything that Republican Man stands for, I had, in the past, smiled and waved to him every week, in that curious and duplicitous way I do in order to keep the peace.

But now it was postelection . . . and all bets were off, baby! This time around, when we entered the dojo, Republican Man jutted out his chin as if to say, "Haha! You're a frustrated liberal loser!" I could have killed him on the spot with my bare hands. But I didn't need to, because class was starting and George had to spar with Republican Man's son.

As I stood and watched, I became aware that I was projecting every ounce of sublimated rage I'd held inside for the past four years onto innocent children. I looked over at Republican Man, and in my infinite hausfrau wisdom, I thought, Ah, you know, we're all human beings. I need to love and accept this man and thus begin the healing our country so desperately needs. And then I thought, No way! and sent George a telepathic message, which—whether or not it was received—delighted me to my toes.

Six: The Tale of the Note in the Lunch Box

Lynne and I were talking on the phone about the simple pleasure to be found in the act of making lunches for our kids to take to school. She said she loves getting up early to make lunches because it's a way for her to stay connected to them during the day—she can think of them and know that they're eating the good food she prepared. And so I recounted for Lynne "The Tale of the Note in the Lunch Box," which had occurred the week prior and which underscored for me the way I tend to get stuck in certain routines and ideas and ways of being and perceiving myself and others, even though they're not working for me or anyone else for that matter. Sometimes I need a guru, like an eight-year-old boy, for example, to make me see the error of my ways.

Lately I've been getting up really early in the morning to write in my journal for a while before the chaos of the house swirls around me. And, like Lynne, I also enjoy this time to make wholesome lunches for the kids, which is what I do immediately after making a nice big pot of Java Joe's Wicked French Roast, and feeding Shlomo, who twists around my legs like a viper, and watering the plants, and feeding Trippy the turtle, whom I awaken by snapping on the reading lamp (aka "the sun") affixed to his tank.

I'm going to digress here for a moment to say that I'm taking on a whole lotta guilt over this turtle deal. That poor reptile just seems so damn depressed. In the beginning, when my dad gave the turtle to George for his third birthday, Trippy at least used to climb up on his rocks and try to scale the walls of his tank to freedom. The sound of his shell bonking desperately against the glass tank, as his claws slipped down the sides, was regularly heard in our household. But now the poor guy just lies there, sleeping mostly, venturing to the surface only to snap up a few morsels of ReptoMin® turtle food. He also seems to have developed some sort of unholy alliance with his filter, which he frequently mounts. But that's a story for another day.

Back to the lunch-making. It is meditative and lovely. The house is quiet and the sky is still pitch-black. My mind wanders gently, as it is fresh and soft with sleep. I choose healthy foods for George's lunch box first, being careful to disguise them in "cool" containers. I then add a few less healthy and even nutritionally devoid items, which he has requested, being sure to balance them mindfully with the good stuff. It is like a macrobiotic exercise, and I've honed my skills after months of trial and error: What will he eat? What will he shun?

On the morning in question, I felt compelled to include a note to him, which I have done many times before, starting way back when he was in preschool, when I read in one of my parenting books that writing love notes to your child is a quick and yet thoughtful way to make him/her feel more secure and connected to you throughout the day. I loved the idea of George opening up his lunch box and finding the note and reading it. It made my heart go warm and cozy.

Just knowing that George had read the notes used to be enough, but I dunno, lately I've been feeling a mounting insecurity about my mothering skills, since my existence has shifted away from the nuts-and-bolts duties of survival (e.g., nursing an infant and changing diapers) to the gut-wrenching, abstract vocation of providing unconditional love and emotional support as my eight-year-old navigates the rocky terrain of second grade and the incredibly fucked-up world beyond.

And when I feel insecure about the job I'm doing, I start fishing around for validation, a trait I picked up from my father and that I have chided him about on many occasions.

And so, when George got home from school, I asked him if he had seen the note in his lunch box. And though I knew in my heart of hearts what George was thinking—he was clearly struggling internally, I could tell, because he didn't want to hurt my feelings—I was unable to let it go or control myself.

Then it all slammed into me at once. The loss of innocence! My boy is growing up and has suddenly become self-conscious in front of his peers (the little bastids)! Furthermore, my feeble attempts to connect with him are no longer cutting the mustid!

Torturing myself, I imagined the lunchroom scene. Not only had I embarrassed my son in front of his friends, but then I had to go and try to make myself feel better by needing him to validate *me*! Oh God! The loss! The pain in my heart!

I felt as though I was being eviscerated by a pack of wild dogs. However, I had enough presence of mind to try to listen to my son, an exercise that never seems to get any easier for me, no matter how many times I perform it.

But I did it: I sat with the discomfort and the loss I was feeling, and was richly rewarded moments later, when George taught me everything I needed to know about this particular blunder—and then some.

Seven: The Tale of Natural Consequences

IF YOU YELL AT YOUR KIDS, YOU MIGHT AS WELL GO AHEAD AND HIT THEM. IT DOES THE SAME AMOUNT OF DAMAGE.

PAM LEO
PARENT EDUCATOR

OOPS.

NATURAL CONSEQUENCES!
• no preservatives
• no hormones
• no dyes
• no artificial colors
THEY'RE GOOD FOR YOU!

DORA!
NUDIST/PERFORM-ANCE ARTIST-IN-RESIDENCE

Craig and I took a parenting workshop[1] when George was four and Dora was a wee babe and it had become clear—as clear as an azure sky in the deepest summer—that we couldn't fake it anymore. We really didn't have any idea what the hell we were doing in the parenting department and we possessed zero tools with which to do it, other than the occasional, short-lived escapes provided by heavy drinking.

In the workshop, we learned that when it comes to discipline, spanking is a big no-no, which we'd kinda already deduced, and so is yelling at your kids. What works best is providing consistent rules and "natural consequences" for behavior.

For example, let's just hypothetically say that our four-year-old daughter has recently developed a passion for graffitiing our floors and walls and also her body and clothing (when I can get her to wear clothing, that is) with permanent marker. Even though we've provided her with a li'l artist's easel, reams of paper on which to create, and washable paints and markers, and we've articulated the rules about vandalism clearly and repeatedly, the "natural consequences for behavior" part of the equation gets a little murky because:

1. I'm never actually able to catch her in the act because she is so stealthy, and no matter where I hide my black Sharpies, she's able to sniff them out and use them to silently deface our property; and

---

1. Pam Leo, who taught the class, is excellent—and so is her book, *Connection Parenting*.

2. Her graffiti, which she refers to as her "work," often includes my name, too, which she has just very proudly learned how to write and has committed to memory, and I am secretly touched that she thinks of me so often that I have become part of her "work," as it were; and

3. She is so earnest about her work and loves her art supplies so much that I feel like a shrill and callous, blind adult who cares more about pristine walls than the passion in a brushstroke; and also

4. She's so damn cute that it nearly kills me.

Still, I know intellectually that I should not be allowing my daughter to besmirch our walls and floors and her clothing and body in this manner, so I cling to the guidelines we learned in our parenting workshop, repeatedly stating, "The rule is that we draw and paint on paper, not on the walls/floors/clothing/your body." And then I remind her of the consequence—the natural consequence, that is—which is that if she vandalizes our home again, she will lose her art supplies for the rest of the day. And when I say this, her face breaks and she sobs and wails and the tears well up in her eyes, and I wonder, What the hell should I do now?

Eight: The Tale of the Dunkin' Donuts Drive-Thru Debacle

SINK FULL OF DIRTY DISHES

STACK OF OVERDUE BILLS

DIRTY LAUNDRY

IMPROPERLY SHOD DAUGHTER

BURNT-ON SCHMUTZ ON STOVE

WHITE PAINT

CANS OF PAINT

TO DO TODAY:
- groceries
- sign G up for indoor baseball
- sign Dora up for next dance class
- Paint store: 2 gallons eggshell
- pet store: turtle food, new filter
- ice skates for kids
- call City Hall
- birthday presents for kids
- pay parking tix
- babysitter for Friday night
- clean house: mom + dad visit?

he day started like any other.
I awoke to the heaping piles of unfinished business and other people's crap that lay about the house, and so I rolled up my sleeves and made a big pot of coffee, drank it, and then became a jittery, scattered, over-whelmed shrew unable to deal with any of it.

One of the many items on my to-do list was to get Dora the Mary Jane shoes she'd been asking for for months. Seeing that the temp had begun to dip into the 30s the previous two nights and the only footwear that fit my daughter's feet was a pair of much-beloved strappy sandals, I decided to blow off the urgent house-hold responsibilities and drive around looking for a store that carried Mary Janes.

We drove from shoe store to shoe store to shoe store for over three hours, looking for the Mary Janes that Dora had her heart set on—to no avail. Since both of our blood-sugar levels were starting to plummet, and because I wouldn't have any money left over with which to purchase my daughter's shoes if we stopped and had a real lunch, I decided to go through the Dunkin' Donuts drive-thru to get a large coffee with cream and sugar to stave off my hunger and also to pick up a doughnut for Dora, who'd requested just such a treat.

When we pulled up to the drive-thru's ordering microphone, Dora began to shriek like a banshee when I ordered her a maple-frosted with sprinkles, which confused me because that's what she always wants when she and I have the pleasure of patronizing Dunkin' Donuts together.

Her screams shot through my body and I whirled my head around, yelling for her to be quiet in a voice so guttural and horrible that it scared even me. Needless to say, my most regrettable parenting moment to date was broadcast through the Dunkin' Donuts loudspeaker, and the cashier who handed me my spoils gave me a look that said, You don't deserve that child.

And I had to agree. For the time being, anyway.

I roared out of the drive-thru in the Subaru and pulled over in the parking lot next door, where I wept and shook and realized I had visited a deep, dark place—deeper and darker indeed than anywhere I had yet visited as a mother.

The Inferno

Nel mezzo del cammin di nostra vita
mi ritrovai per una selva oscura
ché la diritta via era smarrita.
                    —Dante, *The Inferno*, Canto One

(Midway upon the journey of our life
I found myself within a forest dark,
For the straightforward pathway had been lost.)

B ut I was to visit a deeper and darker place in short order: a place populated by souls so wretched and grotesque that it made my hair stand on end. It was a place like no other. It was the realm of people who need to be severely punished.

My Descent into the Realm of the People Who Need to Be Severely Punished

ante came to me the next night and took me by the hand and led me down, down, down into the depths of the Earth, through the nine circles of hell, past the slothful and the greedy souls, the fraudulent and the violent souls, past the guideposts announcing crimes of increasing wickedness, until we arrived at the very center of the Earth. It was a hausfrau inferno. I was sweating bullets!

After passing by the terrifying she-monster guarding the entrance, I immediately recognized the morbidly obese man from the Westbrook playground who stands around drinking beer and smoking cigarettes, ignoring his own filthy juvenile delinquent offspring and instead ogling the butts of and commenting on the parenting choices of the mothers gathered there. A few years before, he'd admonished me for letting my teething daughter chew on a wood chip. Although I didn't say so to Dante, I was thrilled to see his fat ass down there, getting his comeuppance.

---

1. "Abandon all hope, ye who enter here."

Also there, roasting in the hellfire, was the wrinkled and depleted old lady who bitched at me for letting George play in the revolving door at the Portland International Jetport while we waited near the luggage carousel after a twelve-hour day of travel from visiting my sister Boo in Seattle.

And there, too, was the pimply Goth teenager who, while showing off in front of his friend, made a disparaging remark about my parenting when I lost my cool in front of the Portland Public Market and shouted at George to stop kicking his sister's car seat.

Also present among the damned was the gross old man who cupped his hands around his mouth and screamed "Terrorist lovers!" at me and the kids and the other people who were gathered in Monument Square to protest the Iraq War on International Women's Day.

I also noticed that the man who designed the point-of-purchase candy rack for grocery store checkout lines was there, shoveling coal into a fiery pit.

And so was the person who thought it was a good idea to use arsenic-leaching pressure-treated wood in playgrounds and parks across America.

And then there was that middle-aged man who appeared out of nowhere when I was exiting the grocery store with two crabby children and a cart spilling over with groceries, and who made a comment suggesting that I looked overwhelmed but did not actually offer to assist me in any way. He'd disappeared just as quickly through the automatic sliding glass doors after sharing his shrewd observation.

And then there was the ice cream truck guy, the well-disguised hawker of frozen toxins, who summons innocents with his siren song, a Casiotone rendition of the first four bars of Scott Joplin's "The Entertainer." He plays it over and over and over again—a technique so effective that even Dora, when she was eighteen months old, would run through the house screaming "Bah-baahh!" (her word for Popsicle) whenever the ungodly notes were struck, which always seemed to be right before lunch, right before dinner, and at bedtime.

Craig and I made a big mistake when we allowed the kids to purchase a couple of hyperactivity-inducing Popsicles one early summer eve, caught up, as we were, in romantic memories of our own childhood summer treats, forgetting that once a child tastes this man's wares, you can never go back!

And then I saw Jim Keithley, an editorialist for the *South Portland–Cape Elizabeth Sentry*, who was bothered by a mother breastfeeding her daughter at a town council meeting. He wrote, "Maybe I was the only one in the room who noticed. I'm not sure. Maybe next time, Mom could keep her breasts tucked in and take her daughter to McDonald's for a Happy Meal. At least that meal comes with a toy." I was sure glad to see him roasting away in a skanky and fetid McDonald's bathroom stall.

I also saw the childless old worrywart who voluntarily projected her own fears about germs and shoelessness onto my daughter, when Dora and I were helping plant potatoes at a local farm.

Also there, in the fiery depths, was the Over-Protective-Know-It-All Mother (O.P.K.I.A.M.) from the Deering Oaks playground, who apparently wasn't satisfied by trying to micromanage every nanosecond of her own child's existence, but also found it necessary to weigh in with mine. When George and his friends climbed to the top of the jungle gym, which they had done many times and which I condoned, the O.P.K.I.A.M. let loose an absurd remark that made me want to give her a huge shove.

And speaking of miserable killjoys with acronyms, the real queen of the damned was there, too: the one known only as the Unbelievably Irritating Nosy Bitch from Massachusetts (U.I.N.B.M.). The kids and I had first encountered her when Dora was two and a half and wearing big-girl undies and going poop and pee-pee in her little potty but was still not what you'd call experienced in bladder control, meaning that we'd had quite a few urinary accidents (the frequency of which was inversely proportional to my ability to remember to leave the house with a change of clothes for her).

I'd taken the kids to Kettle Cove Beach for an afternoon of digging in the sand and frolicking in the leg-numbing surf. And there she was—the U.I.N.B.M., spending her afternoon in a beach chair, scowling at me and my offspring from over the top of the best-selling novel she was clutching between her bony knees and shriveled teats. I was being my usual distracted self, trying to keep track of George, who kept disappearing around the jagged rock face he was scaling while pretending to be a Revolutionary War hero.

Suddenly, Dora tugged desperately at my tankini, trying to alert me to the fact that she needed to "go pee-pee in the potty," which was conveniently located down the beach, over the bridge, through the grassy path, and behind the trees on the other side of the parking lot. Because her bladder was in no way capable of the control necessary to make that lengthy trek, I made the quick yet sound decision to let her peel off her bathing suit bobbins[2] and go pee-pee right there on the beach, where the gentle surf met the sand.

A much-relieved Dora did just that, squatting low and wide with the gusto and concentration of a woman about to give birth. Though I was standing in front of her to discreetly block her from the gazes of nearby beachgoers, I could feel the glare of the U.I.N.B.M. boring into my back. When I turned around to assist Dora in the pulling-up of her bobbins, I locked eyes with the U.I.N.B.M., who then felt compelled to shrilly condemn my daughter's behavior.

I remained calm on the outside and modeled peaceful coexistence to my daughter, but on the inside I was a boiling cauldron of rage, and I fully fantasized about verbally crushing the heinous wretch before bludgeoning her senseless with her copy of *The Da Vinci Code*.

Boy, was I glad to see her shriveled ass frying away down there, in the hausfrau inferno! Thanks, Dante!

2. bobbins (bobbinth). *n*: bottoms. [Middle toddler.]

A Girlfriend for Hausfrau

ne eve, a few years ago now, I received an e-mail from my friend John, in San Francisco, alerting me to a telephone conversation he'd had earlier that day with George while I was out:

> Dearest Nic,
> Just thought you'd want to know that today George answered the phone when I called and he and I had an interesting little chat. Here's how it went:
> George: Why don't you have a girlfriend?
> John: Because I like boys.
> George: But if you get a girlfriend, she'll do all the cooking and cleaning so you can read the newspaper and watch TV.

Let it be known that this here hausfrau was thrown for a colossal loop. Where the hell did my kid come up with these ideas? I racked my brain for answers. I mean, come on! Haven't I been busting big ass to model an image of woman as strong, independent, sassy, and domestically disinclined? Aren't I "rad" enough? Our tenant is a Wiccan, for God's sake! I have a tattoo! And gay friends!

The fact was, though, that the damage had already been done. And it was my job to talk some sense into my budding sexist.

I wanted to choose a time when we both felt relaxed and comfortable. I'd read in one of my parenting books that that's important when broaching "difficult" subjects with children. Instead, I burst out of the computer room and hunted my six-year-old down like a starving hawk on the trail of an injured field mouse.

I found him in the playroom, shooting Lego pieces at Dora's dollhouse with a rubber band. I took a deep breath, entered the playroom, and told him that we needed to talk. George took off his sunglasses. We sat on the couch together, and I calmly told him that we needed to get a few things straight.

First, I explained that John had e-mailed me about their conversation, and that I was concerned because it appeared that he (George) was misguided in his thinking that women are supposed to do all the cooking and cleaning in the household. I also mentioned that it was rude to assume that John should have a girlfriend, since some boys like girls, but some boys like girls *and* boys, and some girls like boys, but some girls like girls *and* boys, and some girls like other girls, and some boys like just boys.

Of course, George shot back at me without missing a beat.

The incident got me to thinking. Was George right? Did I need a girlfriend? Huh? Did I?

Yes! I did!

I needed a girlfriend. I *wanted* a girlfriend. I wanted a girlfriend more, in fact, than a three-hour chunk of undisturbed reading time. More than being able to complete a phone call without having to lock myself in the bathroom so I can hear. More than a bag of opium and a vibrator.

But don't get your hopes up. I'm not talking about hot lesbo sex here. What I'm talking about is a true-blue Thelma and Louise[1]–style soul sister with whom I can let it all hang out. A woman who has been to the sweet as well as the dark places of motherhood and isn't afraid to be honest about it. A woman with whom I can talk on the phone while urinating and then also flush the toilet afterward—without the slightest disruption in conversational flow. A woman with whom I can *laugh*.

What a huge relief: laughter. But you don't just find that kind of soul sister walking down the street every day. You can try. And try I do, scouring the playgrounds, the preschool drop-off and pickup areas, the play groups, the play table at O'Naturals—you know, all the typical hausfrauian haunts. I always look for a hausfrau who falls somewhere near me on the spectrum of mothering types. I think I land somewhere on the left of this spectrum, but really, all I'm trying to do is make it through the freakin' day most of the time—and I like a gal who can laugh with me on the journey.

Once I find a hausfrau of my liking, I then move quickly into the "courtship" phase, in which I try really hard to make a good impression so that she'll be intrigued and want to take me home—for a playdate, during which frozen yogurt tubes will be consumed and the children will yell and work out their shit in the sandbox.

1. Minus the driving-into-the-Grand-Canyon part.

THE SCENARIO	ON FIRST DATE, YOU:	AT HOME ALONE W/ KIDS, YOU:
"MOMMY! GEORGE CALLED ME AN IDIOT!"	CALMLY REFOCUS THEIR PLAY	YELL," KNOCK IT OFF OR YOU'LL LOSE TV FOR A WEEK."
"MOMMY! I WANT SOME CANDY!"	OFFER A BUNCH OF FRESH, FAIR TRADE ORGANIC GRAPES	BREAK OUT M&M'S AND EAT MOST OF THE BAG YOURSELF
"MOMMY! I HAVE TO GO PEE-PEE!"	SAY, "LET'S GO TO THE POTTY TOGETHER."	SAY," YOU CAN GO IN THE GRASS IN BACK OF THAT TREE."

She and I drink coffee and sit together at the picnic table, trying not to intervene too much. I take part in all the normal first-date fumbles: nervous conversation meant to fill uncomfortable silences, the impulse to appear calm and centered and patient (even though my head feels like it is about to explode), sweaty palms, etc. And I try really hard to be a good mom—employing all the techniques Craig and I learned in our parenting workshop.

I never once yell at my kids or feed them unwholesome snacks in front of the hausfrau I am trying to woo. That would just be a big turn-off. Speaking of turn-offs, one thing I've learned in my many attempts at hausfrau courtship is that having birthed a baby does not a soul mate make!

But then, there's also the gallery of turn-ons. Here's what gets me hot:

A mama who knows just what to do in a moment of difficulty and doesn't make a big deal about it.

A mama who can laugh when she has baby vomit running down her back.

A mama who isn't afraid of appearing vulnerable once in a while.

Once my newfound girlfriend and I start to relax a bit around each other and let go of the self-conscious posturing, the good vibes abound, and the stories start to flow. I just love a hausfrau who can turn a potentially embarrassing scenario into a moment of connection. My knees go absolutely weak for a gal who can weave a good tale that illuminates the hilarity in parenthood.

The absolute hottest of all is when I'm at play group and I get some three-on-one action with my girlfriends Lynne, Delia, and Leah—such as last Tuesday, when we lingered over coffee while the girls broke into Raizel's costumes and dressed Oscar up like a mermaid. Delia told us the following:

> Oh my God, you guys! You're not going to believe what happened this weekend, when Al and I got to spend a few hours together when his folks took the kids. It was Saturday afternoon, you know, and we were going to go out to dinner, so I took a shower—and when I came out, Al and I talked about it and decided not to go out to eat but to stay home and just enjoy our space without the kids.
>
> Al got all amorous, and when I walked into the bedroom, he was standing there, holding back the bedcovers for me. I noticed that there was this big brown streak in the middle of the bed—it was so gross! It was unmistakable and lying there, and I said, "What the hell is _that_?" And it was so funny because Al just shrugged his shoulders and said, "It's OK, I sniffed it. It's not crap. We're good to go."

The Atonement

"Atonement (*at-one-ment*) consists in no more than the abandonment of that self-generated double monster—the dragon thought to be God (superego) and the dragon thought to be Sin (repressed id). But this requires an abandonment of the attachment to ego itself, and that is what is difficult."

How It Came to Be that I Was Bitch-Slapped by the Parenting Gods in the Seasonal Aisle of CVS

Each autumn, as Halloween approaches, I resolve afresh to get my act together and not succumb to the paralyzing sense of dread that the rapidly shortening days engender in me. This year, armed with a newfound ability to hang on to the scant serotonin molecules that my brain manages to produce,[1] I decided that I would begin helping my children prepare for Halloween a bit in advance of the actual holiday, rather than waiting until sunset on October 31 and then scrambling to throw costumes, candy, and trick-or-treat bags together in a slipshod fashion, as I have every Halloween before.

Unfortunately for me, bad karma still lingered from Halloween several years ago, and I was about to experience some wrathful payback from the parenting gods.

But first there was the matter of Dora's costume, which I mistakenly thought would be easy to put together because, since June, she'd repeatedly stated that she wanted to be a pumpkin for Halloween—just like she'd been for the previous three years. With that in mind, the two of us ventured over to the St. John Street Goodwill, an establishment that I ♥ because its downtrodden façade masks a multitude of riches.

---

1. Thank you, Lexapro! That's right: Lexapro, the wonder drug that I take to battle premenstrual dysphoric disorder as well as seasonal affective disorder. With Lexapro, when it's fall or winter and I have my period, I am now merely a bitch and no longer a psychotic bitch from hell.

It's a real reward for those of us who abandon our children in the "toy area" among the piles of twisted, discolored, and oft-shorn Barbie dolls and plastic bags full of forlorn action figures from Happy Meals of yesteryear—still dappled with the greasy french-fry fingerprints of so many tiny hands—so that we bargain hunters can rummage through rack after rack, finding thrift-shop scores galore, like the half-crazed hausfraus we are.[2]

At the Goodwill, my daughter and I hit the jackpot: a whole circular rack of Halloween costumes, right smack dab in the middle of the floor. I could have done a cartwheel right then and there, I was so excited to see that one of the costumes was, in fact, a pumpkin. And let me just clarify that when my daughter said she wanted to be a "pumpkin," what she actually meant was "jack-o'-lantern"—which I intuited with my keen hausfrauian ability to interpret what my children actually mean when they say one thing but intend another. It's a hausfrau's way of knowing!

Anyway, the costume in question included not only a jack-o'-lantern shirt but also a little orange cap with a green stem and leaf attached to the top—which at first glance appeared perfect—so I aggressively snatched that sucker up and turned my back to block the elderly, mustachioed woman who was hobbling toward us, just in case she thought she could lay her mitts on our spoils.

2. Okay. Fully crazed.

In so doing, I noticed that the costume looked a tad small and also that the jack-o'-lantern shirt was not really a shirt at all but was more of a bunting[3] and was probably more appropriate as a Halloween getup for a five-month-old (or a five-year-old without legs).

But because at this point Dora was jumping up and down and screaming—and because the old hobbling woman was looking at me with an expression that seemed to shout, "Ya gonna eat that?"—I hightailed it over to the cash register to pay for the costume, stopping only to rummage through a box of 59-cent swimming goggles and a big wire caddy full of Halloween masks and hats, which was pure pleasure because the kids had been asking for swimming goggles all summer and because I also scored one of those tall, fuzzy, and slightly floppy Dr. Seuss hats, which I believed would be the perfect Halloween costume for Craig.

Dammit, I thought, I'll *make* that jack-o'-lantern bunting fit my daughter! And so I paid the elfin Goodwill man behind the counter, and Dora and I hurried home to make the necessary alterations. The process involved me cutting off the bottom of the bunting to create an opening through which Dora could step into the costume.

3. "A snug-fitting, hooded sleeping bag of heavy material for infants. [Perhaps from Scots *buntin*, plump, short.]"—*The American Heritage Dictionary of the English Language*

She was thrilled with it until she looked through a photo album from the previous year and saw a picture of herself with her kitten, Gray Boy, of whom she is no longer the custodial parent,[4] and she decided to change her costume to reflect her melancholy.

Because I am such an accommodating mother, I indulged Dora's change of heart—after first attempting to guilt[5] her into remaining a pumpkin by underlining the fact that we'd just spent a great deal of time and energy hunting down and modifying the costume she was currently wearing. Not to be deterred by guilt, however, my daughter came up with a perfect compromise, which I thought demonstrated impressively advanced creative problem-solving skills. George, however, did not share my opinion.

---

4. After a series of excruciating tests at the allergist's the winter before, during which I was required to hold George down while a deceitful and morbidly obese nurse repeatedly jabbed needles into his arm, thereby injecting every allergen known to man into his tiny body, we learned that he is allergic to cats as well as dogs, tree pollen, dust mites, mold, grass, and girls. Consequently, Shlomo and Dora's kitten, Gray Boy—whom she'd gotten for Christmas—had to go bye-bye. She did, however, retain visitation rights.

5. One of the most effective—albeit shameful and manipulative—weapons in my parenting arsenal, imparted to me by my dad.

I began to operate on the assumption that on All Hallows Eve my daughter would be dressing up as a kitty inside of a pumpkin—a highly conceptual costume, indeed, which clearly baffled the elderly and irritated the crap out of George, who had recently begun to use the word "freak" as a descriptor for just about everybody in the world except himself.

See, George had a much more back-to-basics Halloween costume in mind—one that was in line with the spirit of the days of yore, when the whole point of Halloween was not about being cute or cuddly but was flatly about scaring the bejesus out of people. Even my son's costuming that year followed a trajectory—one that began with despondence and then, after some prodding by the true-blue stage mother that I am, morphed into a manifestation of his deep feelings of betrayal after Johnny Damon defected[6] from the Red Sox to the Yankees, and then, following a serendipitous visit to CVS, settled firmly into the realm of the grotesque and horrifying.

6. Thank you, Mr. Damon, for causing me to have to explain what the term "sellout" means to my son, who is now so disillusioned that he refuses to turn the pages of his book *Curse Reversed: The 2004 Red Sox* because he's afraid he'll come across your filthy mug.

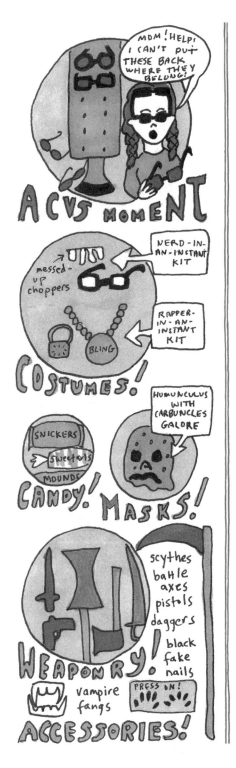

It all came together later that afternoon, in the seasonal aisle, where we were loitering while waiting for my Lexapro prescription to be filled. And will somebody please tell me why it takes half an hour for the pharmacy to fill a prescription if they already have all the drugs right there? Is it so that hausfraus and their offspring have to wait around in the seasonal aisle, *conveniently* located near the pharmacy, just past the cold medicine and spinning rack of sunglasses with which Dora is obsessed? She feels compelled to try on each and every pair of sunglasses, and then is unable to put them back where they belong because the holes where the ear pieces go are too tiny and close together for a preschooler to navigate.

Not to mention the seasonal aisle itself, which is like some sort of bizarre postmodern homage to holiday consumerism, with a dose of toxic foodstuffs thrown in for good measure, guaranteed to have kids whipped up into a lather of desire and pterodactyl-like shrieking in mere moments! I've come to think of our neighborhood CVS as a museum of sorts—and the seasonal aisle as an interactive gallery, if you will, of artifacts lovingly crafted by the Chinese out of plastic and requiring batteries, sure to be coming soon to a landfill near you.

The best part was that the admission to CVS that day cost nothing more than the $25 co-pay for my Lexapro plus the $7.99 I spent on George's Halloween mask and the $5.99 I spent on Dora's *My Little Pony* coloring book (with crayons!) so that she wouldn't feel left out.

The most entertaining battery-operated artifact we saw that day in CVS was this Wolfman Jack–style werewolf character perched atop a miniature Harley, which throbbed and hummed and sang a rendition of "Bad Moon Rising." The kids were enthralled and roared so loudly with laughter that the CVS store manager came down the aisle to "check in" with me and make sure that everything was OK. I assured him that it was. But I was lying.

I was totally tripping out on a flashback I was having that transported me to my college days in the eighties, when my roommates and I got really stoned and went to see David Lynch's *Eraserhead* at the local art-film emporium. The feeling I experienced while struggling to make sense of Lynch's film—part fascination, part repulsion, part identification, part rejection—was bubbling up inside me again as I stood in the seasonal aisle of CVS with my wee ones, the only difference being that now there weren't any mind-altering drugs involved.[7]

But anyhoo, we laughed and frolicked among the artifacts while waiting for my scrip (that's doctor lingo for "prescription") to be prepared, and I gotta admit that I was starting to tweak a little bit and wondered if it was Old Man Gower[8] behind the pharmacy window, counting out my Lexapro pills one by one with his palsied, arthritic, and unsteady hand.

---

7. Except for the one we were currently waiting for the pharmacy to prepare.

8. The geriatric pharmacist from *It's a Wonderful Life*, our favorite holiday movie of all time.

Then George's eye fell on the item that would inspire a fit of begging and pleading and howling and jumping up and down, sprung from the instantaneous belief that this ghoulish accessory would make his Halloween costume—and also his *life*—complete. I speak, of course, of the SCREAM MASK™ WITH BLOOD AND PUMP!

We'd had the privilege, years before—when George was five and had dressed up for Halloween as the Red Power Ranger—of seeing the SCREAM MASK™ WITH BLOOD AND PUMP in action. It was worn by a nine-year-old boy from the neighborhood, whom I had harshly judged (as some sort of psychopath), along with his mother (as some sort of irresponsible dummy with extremely poor judgment), for corrupting my sweet, pure, and innocent boy. See, I had mistakenly thought that my son would have been as repulsed and terrified as I was by the SCREAM MASK™ WITH BLOOD AND PUMP, but, in fact, his silence at the door while we handed out candy was an indication of his great esteem for both the boy and the mask. I suppose the cogs in his mind began to whir even then, and here we were, several years later, and it was time for some serious Hausfrau payback!

I guess I was pretty flippin' naïve back in early 2000 not to have gotten it into my befuddled noggin that judging another parent or child like that was hausfrau hubris of the worst sort, and that such behavior would be duly punished . . . all in good time.

And so it was.

Because if you think that George's fit of howling and begging and moaning and jumping up and down and my eventual acquiescence to buying the SCREAM MASK™ WITH BLOOD AND PUMP out of sheer embarrassment at his behavior got me off the hook, you're sadly mistaken. No, the parenting gods really reamed me by making sure that my caving in to George set off a chain reaction of wanting in my children—and in myself, too, I must admit,[9] which always happens when I go to CVS. So, for the next ten minutes I found myself engaged in an argument with my elder child about whether or not I would also buy him a scythe[10] to complete the grim reaper outfit he was envisioning—an argument which was diverted at times by my younger child, who was also asserting her desires and had begun grabbing seemingly random items from the shelves and shrieking that she wanted them.

9. I forgot to mention before that I bought a few items for myself that day, in addition to my Lexapro, including a set of black press-on nails, which were on sale for $1.99; some Naturtint® hair color, as I was currently sporting a gray stripe down my part that was so striking I could have easily been a skunk for Halloween; and a *People* magazine, so I could revel in some schadenfreude while reading all about Britney Spears, a mother even worse than I.

10. Is it just me, or do you think that the fact that you can buy a six-foot-tall plastic scythe at CVS is proof that Armageddon is nigh?

The Passion of the Hausfrau 193

Actually, it was less of a shriek and more a hybrid of a loud whine and a persistent demand, which, in combination with her brother's fervent pleas for the scythe, sent my head a-spinning. Right then and there it dawned on me that I was receiving A GOOD OLD-FASHIONED BITCH-SLAP FROM THE PARENTING GODS!

I did what any self-respecting hausfrau would do in this situation. I walked away from my loud children and headed over toward the pharmacy counter, where I practiced some deep breathing and humbled myself to the parenting gods, stopping just short of getting down on my knees in front of the spinning rack of sunglasses. Soon I noticed that the clouds had parted and a ray of sunshine beamed down from on high, illuminating the pharmacy window with a celestial light.

Lo and behold, my prescription was ready, and so I gathered my charges and we paid for our sundries. And—but for one last episode at the register involving a struggle over a tin of curiously strong peppermints and a pack of gum[12]—we piled into the Subaru and made our way home, where the serious costuming was about to begin and where the ingredients for that night's dinner lay waiting for me to prepare.

---

11. Except for Tom Cruise.

12. Look, I have nothing against using Altoids and gum to bribe my children into compliance, and indeed it was tempting to allow my children to reach out and grab the sugary treats from the rack under the counter where they lay gleaming. But I have learned from experience that tampering with my children's blood-sugar levels on empty stomachs at 5:15 on a weeknight—although it might afford me several moments of relative quiet as the packs were opened and the sucking and chomping commenced—would be tantamount to giving them crack cocaine.

Halloween was still a few days away, but the kids were primed to begin the festivities immediately, and as I went into the kitchen to pour myself a nice big glass of Côtes de Ventoux[13] and start cookin', they went about costuming themselves, each in their own particular fashion. George tore into the cardboard-and-plastic packaging of his SCREAM MASK™ WITH BLOOD AND PUMP a tad too aggressively and then howled when it appeared that the tubing that is meant to circulate the "blood" out of the pump and up over the mask had snapped in two (see Fig. 1). Between repeated pleas for me to help him make a scythe (Fig. 2), he also found it necessary to enlist my help in finding a plain black cloak (Fig. 3) and went on to instruct me in the finer points of cloakage vs. capeage (Fig. 4).

13. This dangerously inexpensive and suspiciously tasty wine became pretty much a daily habit for me from October through December, prompting me—once the holidays were over, of course—to declare January "Be-Kind-to-My-Liver Month" and stay off the sauce.

Meanwhile, his five-year-old sister disappeared into the recesses of our home, where she'd squirreled away hats, cosmetics, costumes, and accessories (e.g., ladybug antennae she'd fashioned out of a hairband, masking tape, pipe cleaners, and beads), reappearing every few minutes to announce that she'd changed her mind again on the costume front and then parading through the kitchen in several different getups.

I noticed that she seemed to be working through some sort of insect theme. She finally settled on a monarch-butterfly costume, which was especially striking from the neck up, as she'd used the black tempera paint that comes in the little pots on her easel to completely cover her face, creating a minstrely effect, which she seemed pleased with. Dora's metamorphosis was complete at 5:52 p.m., which gave her a few minutes to locate George's skeleton gloves with blood running through them.

I soon heard Craig's truck grinding up the driveway, and I decided that our Halloween dress rehearsal would not be complete without an audience. I put down the spoon with which I had been stirring our evening meal and gathered our tiny troupe together on the couch, so that when Craig walked through the door, exhausted and discouraged by trying to find money to run his non-profit organization, he'd be able to feast his eyes on the *tableau vivant* assembled in our living room.

The parenting gods were smiling down upon us. And it was good.

The Resurrection

Ah, Sun-flower! weary of time,
Who countest the steps of the sun,
Seeking after that sweet golden clime
Where the traveller's journey is done;

Where the Youth pined away with desire,
And the pale Virgin shrouded in snow,
Arise from their graves, and aspire
Where my Sun-flower wishes to go.

—William Blake (1757–1827)

It's a Miracle! Bra!

eorge and Dora are the only ones who'll tell me the truth, and they do so without fail and at all times, like the little hyperactive yin/yang sages that they are. Lately, that truth tends to center around my body: its odors, its imperfections, its myriad signs of deterioration.

Dora likes to hang out in my bedroom and harass me while I dress. She pinches, grabs, lifts, and scrutinizes my body with the enthusiasm of a marine biologist stumbling upon a beached leviathan. Of particular interest to her are my aging skin (which has all the suppleness of an old boot; I can now pinch the skin on the back of my hand and it will stay like that, in pinched formation, for several seconds before sinking back into place) and my boobs (sucked into shriveled oblivion first by George and then Dora, in a nearly uninterrupted six-year breastfeeding stint).

With a spirit of inquiry, Dora sits on the trunk at the end of my bed and watches me, asking questions. Interspersed with her questions come shrewd observations. I can't knock her for using advanced thinking skills, such as metaphor and simile, to describe what she sees. But what really bugs me is the way she draws comparisons between my body and other icky things in the natural world.

The harassment is the worst at the beach, however, here on the rocky coast of Maine, where the distasteful qualities of my nearly forty-year-old bod are exposed to the glare of the sun and provide fodder with which my children may crush—like so many barnacles under their sandals—whatever delusions I've managed to build up about myself.

Like, I thought I looked pretty good in the halter top–style bathing suit I'd purchased at Amaryllis after the perky twenty-something sales clerk assured me that even though there were no "cups" inside the halter top, I could still "totally carry it off" (her words). And, desperate fool that I am, I believed her.

I was desperate because I had been searching in vain for a bathing suit that both fit me and looked good. I ask you: Why are there no attractive bathing suits for forty-year-old women? The only ones I could find that would hold my breasts aloft (with a series of trusses and steel supports) were those horrendously matronly tank-inis with matching skirts, which seem to shout: "I'm covering up the nastiest mess of cellulite and creeping pubic hair you've ever seen in your life!"

And so, when I tried on the halter top–style bathing suit at Amaryllis and the perky clerk told me that I looked "really great," my vanity got the better of me and I bought it. I wore it to the beach the next day with the kids and thought I was looking mighty fine.

But then truth-teller George, trying also to be tactful, looked me over and then set me straight. (See bottom right.)

But enough about the beach. Let's get back to the boobs.

I come from a long line of foremothers who were meaty of thigh and pendulous of breast. Milly was particularly well-endowed. After birthing and nursing three children, her breasts hung clear down to her pelvis. But she celebrated her mammaries and was not at all repulsed by her aging body. She'd get up every morning and go swim a mile at the pool at the Ramada Inn in Mystic, Connecticut, well into her eighties, laughing and shouting as her enormous breasts floated up and bobbed around in the wickedly chlorinated water.

Oh, I wish I could be like Milly and love my God-given teats!

But I'm not like her. I'm too damn vain. I'd like to resurrect my poor li'l puppies and secure them in a position of dignity—somewhere high above my navel.

Enter the Miracle Bra®.

I was first tipped off to its magic one day at work, when I noticed my friend Leanne's drastically improved side view. Her birthday was the week after mine, and this year she'd celebrated by going out and buying herself a Miracle Bra®. At first, I thought she'd gone under the knife. She *had* called out sick the previous week, *hadn't she*?

Leanne calls her breasts her "girls." She explained that for a little over thirty dollars and a trip to the mall, she'd been able to treat her girls to a complete makeover.

After witnessing the results for myself, I quickly followed suit.

I drove over to the mall one afternoon with George, who was under house arrest for being mean to his little sister—and believe me, if there is a seventh circle of hell for a nine-year-old boy, it is the lingerie department at Macy's.

George's punishment quickly morphed into a bliss-fest, however, when he discovered that the waiting nook to which he'd been banished contained a leather couch for sprawling and also a giant plasma-screen TV, broadcasting a Red Sox/Mariners game.

Oh, well. It kept him good 'n' quiet for a really long time while I scoured the racks and racks of bras and tried on one after the other until I found my own perfect miracle: the extreme push-up model Wonderbra® by Maidenform.

I bought three from the daffy old lady at the register, pried my son from the leather couch, and headed home—buoyed by my purchase to new heights of hope and self-confidence, like a middle-aged man behind the wheel of a convertible sports car.

Although technically not a Miracle Bra®—which is only available at Victoria's Secret, a store I gave up patronizing after a ten-minute standoff with George at the entrance—the Wonderbra® has performed bountiful miracles, to which I can attest.

The extreme push-up model has extra padding where I need it most (on top), creating the illusion that my breasts are round—rather than whatever "shape" can be best described as deflated balloons with pebbles at the bottom. My Wonderbra® also is able to produce some nice cleavage as well as the illusion of all-over firmness. If I didn't know better, *I'd* think I had a boob job.

Like Leanne, I've taken to wearing my Wonderbra® to bed at night. It's so nice to look down from my pillow and actually be able to see my breasts there, once again, like the good old days.

And I have been amply rewarded for my purchase. My husband has been more helpful around the house. People I haven't seen in a while stop and stare at my boobs and say, "You look great!" and no doubt wonder if I've been under the knife.

And then there's the most important reward of all: the kudos from my little truth-tellers. But enough of my yakkin'. Behold the miracle for yourself.

---

1. Or should I say "udderly"?

2. Future Wonderbra wearer, circa A.D. 2041.

Part the Third

TRANSITION

"Physical signs of transition include shaking or trembling. . . .
Nausea and vomiting are also common signs. . . . Another physical
sign is the inability to relax or be comfortable. A woman who was
handling labor well may suddenly find that she has no idea
what to do and nothing is comfortable any more."
—www.birthingnaturally.net

The Meeting with the Goddess

"In every system of theology there is an umbilical point, an Achilles tendon which the finger of the mother life has touched, and where the possibility of perfect knowledge has been impaired. The problem of the hero is to pierce himself (and therewith his world) precisely through that point; to shatter and annihilate that key knot of his limited existence."

H is for Hausfrau

ne benefit of pneumonia was that it gave me oodles of undisturbed time to talk on the telephone[1] and read.[2] Those two activities dovetailed one afternoon, when I received a package from my mother, and after opening it, I called Leah to tell her about it.

I told Leah about how Craig had brought the package up to my sickbed and looked at me askance when I opened the priority mailer and pulled a wrapped gift out.

---

1. Pre-pneumonia phone conversations usually involved me locking myself in the bathroom so that I could hear my friend's voice.

2. I'd devoured many books and about ten back issues of *The New Yorker,* which, before I'd gotten sick, had been stacking up on my nightstand, unread. Each week would pass and another *New Yorker* would arrive, and I'd look longingly at the cover and take the magazine upstairs to our bedroom at night to read while putting the kids to bed. I would read half an entry in "Talk of the Town" and then fall asleep myself. In the morning, I'd wake up and *The New Yorker* would have magically disappeared—perhaps some fairies or even Craig had slipped it out of my hands while I was sleeping. I'd later find it in the bathroom, beside the toilet, and I'd read snippets of "Goings on About Town" while urinating. Eventually, I'd take the magazine back to the bedroom and add it to the growing stack, which had become a kind of hausfrau barometer measuring the impossibility of my reading and enjoying a complete aesthetic experience without being interrupted.

It was clearly a book and had a note card from the Edward Gorey House attached: *A little light reading from me and Mr. Gorey to help cheer you up! Love, Mom.*

Craig backed out of the room and left me with my morbid curiosity and my mother's gift, which I tore into. It was a copy of Edward Gorey's *Gashlycrumb Tinies.*[3]

Don't get me wrong: I'm fond of Edward Gorey (may he rest in peace) and have been inspired by his wit, imagination, and drawing ability. So on the one hand, it was sweet that my mother had thought to get me the book. Yet once again, it also opened up another big ouchie in me that I thought had healed but obviously hadn't.

And so I recounted for Leah the tale of the time I took the kids to Cape Cod to visit my folks and my mother led us through the Edward Gorey House, where she volunteers as a tour guide.

---

3. Reveling in the irony, I read aloud for Leah a section of *The Gashlycrumb Tinies*, Edward Gorey's illustrated poem that details alphabetically the deaths of twenty-six children:

A is for Amy who fell down the stairs.
B is for Basil assaulted by bears. . . .
G is for George smothered under a rug . . .

and so on.

Leah patiently listened to me go on and on. And when I paused for a moment, she asked me why I was so angry.

"I guess it's because my own mother doesn't really know who I am," I said. "She knows Edward Gorey and all about his life and his stories, but she doesn't know mine. She doesn't even think of me as a real writer."

"But you *are* a real writer," Leah said.

"Am I?" I said. "How so?"

Look, Hausfrau, you have to let go of your anger toward your mother. It's what's making you sick. Don't forget that the lungs are the seat of grief. You're choosing to hold on to your grief rather than choosing to let it go. You have your own voice now, Hausfrau. So let go of all this crap about your mother and put your good energy into your own story. Be your own mother, if you know what I mean. Tell your own story! Open your mouth and let it come out! Now go and drink some herbs.

So I did. I poured myself a big cup of the herbal infusion from the pot on my nightstand and choked it down. Soon, I fell into another hallucinatory sleep.

dreamed that I was being born. I was coming out of my mother but was still attached to her by the umbilical cord. I found a sword lying on the ground and I sliced myself free. A dragon's head grew out of my belly button, so I cut it off, and then blood spurted out. The red droplets turned white, and then they grew and became sheets of paper. They were my stories, and they all swirled around my head like a crown, before coming to settle back down on the bed and into my journal.

Apotheosis

"If the hero in his triumph wins the blessing of the goddess or the god and then is explicitly commissioned to return to the world with some elixir for the restoration of society, the final stage of his adventure is supported by all the powers of his supernatural patron."

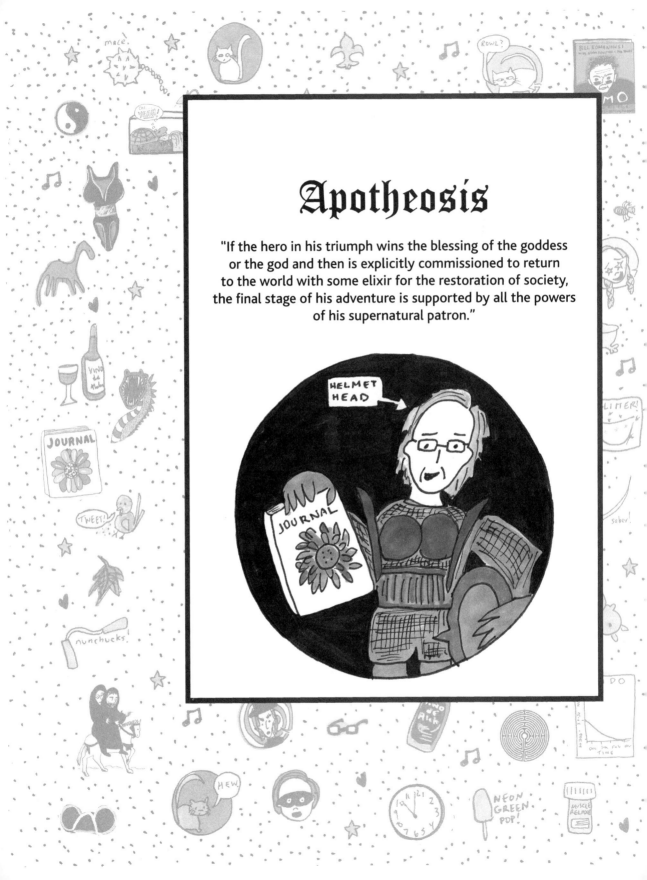

I Am Visited by the Living and the Dead

A wash with fever, sweating, soaking the sheets, a-coughin' and a-peein', I drifted in and out of consciousness. I thought I heard laughter. It was George's laughter—and then I realized the laughter was not coming from a far-off place but rather from right beside me.

George was there, sitting on the floor next to my bed, and he was reading my journal. At first, this made me nervous, so I leaned over to try to grab it out of his hands, but he pulled it away, catching me off guard, as he tends to do.

Then Dora came in and gave me a card she had made for me in the shape of a sun, her love radiating out of it, and it just about broke my heart. I began to sob and sweat more profusely.

And then Craig came in with more herbal infusion. I pulled myself up in bed and visited with them all for a while, sipping on my herbs.

Soon it was time for George to start getting ready for baseball practice, and Craig herded the kids out of the bedroom.

I opened my journal to do some writing and found that I had only a few pages left before the whole journal was filled. I flipped to the last page and discovered that Milly had written out a passage from Walt Whitman's *Specimen Days*, a book she had given me in the way, way, way B.C. days, when I'd graduated from

college. Seeing my grandmother's meticulous handwriting on the page like that gave me a heartache. Goose bumps sprang up on my arms as I read:

A happy hour's command!
Down in the woods . . . If I do it at all I must delay no longer. Incongruous and full of skips and jumps as is that huddle of diary-jottings. . . . The resolution and indeed mandate comes to me this day, this hour—(and what a day! What an hour just passing! The luxury of riant grass and blowing breeze, with all the shows of sun and sky and perfect temperature, never before so filling me, body and soul)—to go home, untie the bundle, reel out diary scraps and memoranda, just as they are, large or small, one after another . . . and let the melange's lackings and wants of connection take care of themselves. It will illustrate one phase of humanity anyhow; how few of life's days and hours (and they not by relative value or proportion, but by chance) are ever noted. Probably another point, too, how we give long preparations for some object, planning and delving and fashioning, and then, when the actual hour for doing arrives, find ourselves still quite unprepared, and tumble the things together, letting hurry and crudeness tell the story better than fine work. At any rate I obey my happy hour's command, which seems curiously imperative. May be, if I don't do anything else, I shall send out the most wayward, spontaneous, fragmentary book ever printed.

—Walt Whitman, July 2, 1882

There it was—right there at the end of my hausfrau journal, Walt Whitman's description of how *his* book came to be. I read Walt's words again, and that's when it hit me: I already have the material for a book—*my* book! A hausfrau book!

And then, under the Walt Whitman quote, Grammy Mil had written:

New York City: The Morgan Library and Museum,
225 Madison Avenue at 36th Street.
The Clare Eddy Thaw Gallery.

I took this to be a sign. I called out to Craig to come quickly.

The Ultimate Boon

"The adventure of the hero represents the moment in his life when he achieved illumination—the nuclear moment when, while still alive, he found and opened the road to the light beyond the dark walls of our living death."

The Morgan Library and Museum

Our journey to New York City began like any other lengthy car trip with the children in the wee hours of the morn, with a delicious yet short-lived chunk of stunned silence (which I mistakenly interrupted[1] by offering up the fried-egg-and-cheese bagel sandwiches I'd prepared hours earlier when I'd arisen and, still feverish and hallucinating, started to worry about what I should pack to eat in the car).

Craig was at the helm of our Subaru Forester. The kids were in the back, strapped into their safety restraints. I drank some of my herbal infusion. After a few moments of chomping and digesting, the protein and carbs in the bagel sandwiches kicked in, providing just the right amount of fuel to spark a nasty fight between the kinder.

The point of contention was a certain coloring book I'd bought for George years before, when he was four and Dora was an infant and both of them had pinkeye. We were hanging around the CVS pharmacy waiting for some prescription eyedrops, and I told George he could choose a treat if he was compliant.

Although he was not in the least bit compliant, he ran over to the toy area—next to the diapers and sippy cups and rectal thermometers—and scaled the racks, ignoring the girls' toys, in search of weaponry. I tried to

---

1. When the hell will I learn to not insert myself in the infrequent quietude of my children?

2. Accompanying us was Shabbat Bear, on loan to us from the kids' Jewish day school.

divit his attention by offering up a "My Li'l Fuzzy Guy" coloring book—which appeared to be the least psychically damaging item on offer—but he would have none of it.

He was determined to leave CVS with a pair of handcuffs (which seemed wrong on so many levels[3]), and my urging of the coloring book only served to inflame his lust for the cuffs. He looked so desperate, with his pink and crusty eyes, begging and pleading for the cuffs, that I totally caved and bought the damn things—and I also purchased the coloring book, just to balance out the bad juju.

Though the cuffs have seen much action over the years, the coloring book has lain at the bottom of our art-supply closet, forlorn and quite forgotten. Until a few days before, that is, when I fell ill and Dora went rummaging through the closet, unguided, and discovered and liberated "My Li'l Fuzzy Guy" (with stickers! and activities!) out from under the heap of scrap paper and egg cartons and empty bottles of tempera paint. She applied crayon to its virgin pages and completed some of the activities ("help My Li'l Fuzzy Guy get through the maze and escape big brother's handcuffs by finding refuge under mama's skirt," etc.) and thus laid claim to the coloring book.

3. Especially the spelling of the word "kuffs."

George couldn't have given a rat's ass about My Li'l Fuzzy Guy—until the very moment we began hurtling down I-95 toward New York City, when he suddenly developed a powerful sentimental attachment to it. The bickering resumed moments after Craig's mighty bellow, and it went on and on and on, until Dora used her creative problem-solving skills and turned the situation around by issuing forth a powerful expletive. Color me an unfit mother for endorsing vulgar language, but I thought Dora's word choice was brilliant, given that the third definition for the word "bastard" in the *American Heritage Dictionary of the English Language* is "a person, especially one who is held to be mean or disagreeable." Even though I was feverish and hallucinating, I can tell you with absolute certainty that at that particular moment, George fit the definition.

Five and a half hours later, we found ourselves on Madison Avenue, at the Morgan Library and Museum—and Grammy Mil must have been right there with us because we pulled into a parking space right in front of the building. I ask you: What are the odds of that?

4. Oy! Vat is the deal vis zis helmsman?

5. Feh! What kind of language is that for a little girl?

Inside, our mouths hung open at the sheer opulence. What a difference several hundred million dollars can make in your decorating budget!

First, there was the glass elevator, which no child (or any of the adults buzzed on the champagne they were pouring at a private function for donors in the lobby) could refuse. George spent well over an hour riding up and down, exclaiming loudly to everyone about the thrill of it all and basking in the magnificence of J.P. Morgan's treasures.

Meanwhile, I followed Milly's words in the journal I was clutching to my chest and found my way over to the Clare Eddy Thaw Gallery, which was this glassed-in soundproof room off the lobby. As I entered, I was immediately calmed and centered by the quiet and stillness. I was drawn like a moth to the flame to a glass case in the middle of the room containing a medieval manuscript from the fifteenth century. It was a book of hours[7] illuminated by the Flemish Master of Guillebert de Mets.

---

6. Oy! I feel loose in the kishkas!

7. The most popular books in the Middle Ages, books of hours were illuminated manuscripts that contained text, prayers, and psalms. Laypeople used them in their daily devotions.

The manuscript was open to a page with text forming the "Oratio de Sancta Margareta," and on the facing page, there was a picture of Saint Margaret of Antioch[8] emerging from a dragon with her joined hands raised in devotion, a halo of light crowning her head. Legend has it that Saint Margaret was swallowed by a dragon, and escaped alive by irritating the dragon's innards with the cross she was carrying.

I was unable to tear my eyes away from the illumination. I have no idea how much time passed as I stood there. A security guard near the door coughed at some point and broke my trance, but only momentarily. He looked at me suspiciously as I opened my journal to the very last page and took out my pen and started to sketch the image.

My reverie went on and on, with me sketching and sweating, transported, so that the glow from Saint Margaret's halo illuminated my own hausfrauian head. I never wanted anything as badly as I wanted to get inside that glass case to turn the pages of the book so that I could see the rest of the drawings. And then George and Dora burst through the door, shouting excitedly for me to come see Mr. Morgan's library.

8. Believers consider St. Margaret a patron saint of pregnancy, labor, and childbirth. She is also considered to be a transformation of the pagan divinity Aphrodite. In the Greek church, Saint Margaret is known as Marina. Her festival is celebrated on July 17. In art, she is usually pictured escaping from a dragon.

They grabbed me by my hands and pulled me out into the lobby, through a marble-floored corridor, and into the grandest room of all, with three tiers of bookcases fashioned of bronze and Circassian walnut and holding thousands of the rarest books in the world, an immense fireplace offset by a sixteenth-century tapestry, and a Gutenberg Bible display.

But the ceiling was what captivated us most. Its vaults and recesses featured intricate portraits of great thinkers (men) surrounded by their muses (women) and signs of the zodiac.

The kids lay down on the floor to look at the ceiling—and they shouted for me to come join them. I couldn't. For I am an adult, and the security guard was watching our every move.

Craig came in after his travels in the great glass elevator and sat next to me on the bench near the fireplace. I opened my journal to show him the image I had sketched of myself as Margaret of Antioch, emerging from the dragon.

The fever and confusion of the past few days had drained out of me. For now, I felt completely clear.

9. Now, that's what I call a ceiling!

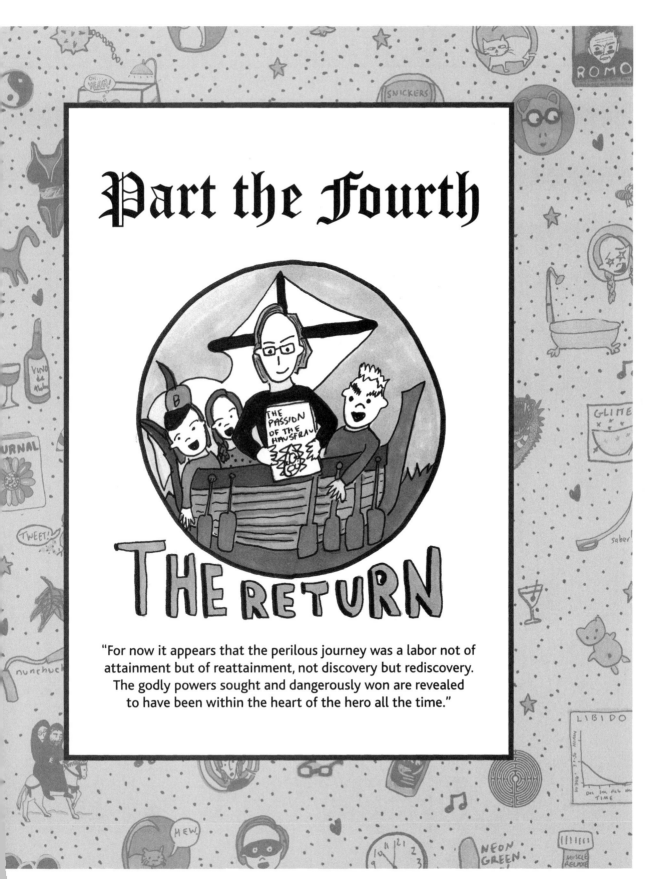

Part the Fourth

THE RETURN

"For now it appears that the perilous journey was a labor not of attainment but of reattainment, not discovery but rediscovery. The godly powers sought and dangerously won are revealed to have been within the heart of the hero all the time."

Crossing of the Return Threshold

"What, now, is the result of the miraculous passage and return?"

Another Friday Night Shabbat Party at Jake and Leah's

One terrific perk of having had pneumonia was that I lost a lot of weight. Subsisting on herbal infusions for the better part of two weeks had paid off. Between the lack of food and my boosted metabolism due to high fevers, I managed to drop almost twenty pounds. And so, the following Friday, when our family arrived at Jake and Leah's for another Friday night Shabbat celebration, I received kudos from the ladies on my trim new look.

Jake was grilling chicken on the porch, and the kids started running around in the backyard, George rallying his troops and Dora and Louisa arguing over a stuffed animal. It felt so good to be back in the fold with our dear friends and familiar sights and sounds!

The ladies and I retired to the back porch after dinner, as we are wont to do, but this time we didn't partake of a clandestine cigarette. Instead, we gabbed and gabbed, catching up on the events of the last few weeks. I waxed lyrical about my hallucinations and revelations, about my grandmother's portents and our trip to New York City, and about *The Passion of the Hausfrau*, which I had realized was pretty much ready to send out into the world.

Wouldn't you just know it: Dr. M said that her college roommate happened to be an editor at a publishing company in New York, and I should send the book to her. So I did.

A Shout on the Beach

Flash forward to the following week. The kids and I were on the beach, enjoying one of those days that makes me roll down the windows in the Subaru and shout "I love Maine!" when we cross over the Casco Bay Bridge into South Portland, on our way to Kettle Cove. The rugosa roses were blooming, there was a salty sea breeze, the sky was azure blue, and the trails and paths at Kettle Cove were soft and romantic and full of bees and birds as we walked to our favorite beach spot, where we could see the lobster boats bobbing and the cormorants plunging.

Dora and I were building an ornate sand castle, and George was creating a moat around us, when my cell phone rang. It was a number I did not recognize, but I decided to answer it anyway, much to George's chagrin. Dora kept working on the castle, but George protested loudly, until he noticed what must have been the ecstatic look on my face.

It was Dr. M's college roommate, the editor from New York, who was calling to thank me for sending her *The Passion of the Hausfrau* and to tell me that she loved it and wanted to publish it. I demurely answered her questions, thanked her for calling me, and hung up. And then I jumped up and down and screamed at the top of my lungs and laughed and whooped and jumped some more, much to my children's embarrassment.

But when I shared my news with them, they too jumped and shouted, and we danced around on the beach together and laughed until we collapsed in the sand.

Later, on our way home from the beach, while the kids were licking their ice cream cones in the backseat, I took a few moments to call Craig and share the good news. Then I called my parents.

My father answered, and we talked for a short while, and he heartily congratulated me and then passed the phone to my mother.

I took a big breath. Then I told her my news, and said I was sorry that I had been such a bitch over the last year or so. And though we'd probably never be selected to participate in a symposium that features mothers and daughters who communicate well, I said I'd come out of the whole pneumonia episode feeling like I wasn't angry at her anymore. Instead, I felt grateful for her gift. I said that I realized that it didn't matter what her intentions were in giving me the gift, since whatever she had given me at that vulnerable spot in my life would have served as a Rorschach test for my soul. Then I said, "Thank you, Mom, for giving me life. And for giving me *Romo: My Life on the Edge: Living Dreams and Slaying Dragons* by Bill Romanowski with Adam Schefter and Phil Towle."

And this is what she said:

Acknowledgments

I wish to thank pretty much everyone, even those who need to be severely punished, for providing me with so much material, support, and encouragement. Extra special thanks go to Dora, George, and Craig; Susan Golomb; Ann Binder; Marnie Cochran, Evan Camfield, and the Random House team; all the dedicated women at PPNNE and FPAM; Ana Sortun; Annette Jolles; Ava Moskin; Ayun Halliday; Boo and Jimmy; Brenda Surabian and Sacopee Valley Midwives; Charlie, Anna, and Emma; China Martens; Chris Iyer; Chris and Lisa Bowe and Stuart and Longfellow Books; Chuck; Dank and Jen; Debra Spark; Deirdre S/M; Delia and Al; Elisa; Jen "Dud" Judd-McGee; Ginny Siegfried; Grace Maselli; *Hausfrau muthah-zine* readers and contributors; Jeremy Hutchins; Jessica Porter; John Vlahides; John, Stacy, and Emma; The Joseph Campbell Foundation; Kate Haas; Leah and Jake and Friday night Shabbat parties; Les and Sam; Leslie Oster; Leticia Plate; Levey Day School; Lori Bess and David; Lunden; Lynne and John; Mac Davis; Margaret and Karl; The Morgan Library and Museum; Peesh Rewak; Portland Stage Company; Rae; Raye Tibbitts; Roberta Bass; Sarah Teres and *Motherwords*; Stona Fitch; and Tom, Cindy, and Doug.

But most of all, Mom and Dad: thank you for giving me life! And thank you for giving me *Romo, My Life on the Edge: Living Dreams and Slaying Dragons* by Bill Romanowski with Adam Schefter and Phil Towle.

Notes

Page numbers follow for quotations taken from Joseph Campbell, *The Hero with a Thousand Faces,* third edition (Novato, California: New World Library, 2008).

Page 1: "The blunder may amount to the opening of destiny." Campbell, page 42.

Page 15: "This fateful region of both treasure and danger . . . is always a place of strangely fluid and polymorphous beings, unimaginable torments, superhuman deeds, and impossible delight." Campbell, page 48.

Page 16: "Freud has suggested that all moments of anxiety reproduce the painful feelings of the first separation from the mother—the tightening of the breath, congestion of the blood, etc. of the crisis of birth." Campbell, page 44.

Page 27: "The call to adventure signifies that destiny has summoned the hero and transferred his spiritual center of gravity from within the pale of his society to a zone unknown. . . . For those who have not refused the call, the first encounter of the hero journey is with a protective figure (often a little old crone) . . . who provides the adventurer with amulets against the dragon forces he is about to pass." Campbell, pages 48 and 57.

Page 35: "Only birth can conquer death—the birth, not of the old thing again, but of something new." Campbell, page 11.

Page 46: "One is harrassed, both day and night, by the divine being that is the image of the living self within the locked labyrinth of one's own disoriented psyche. . . . Here, instead of passing outward, beyond the confines of the visible world, the hero goes inward, to be born again." Campbell, pages 50 and 77.

Page 53: "The hero is the man of self-achieved submission. But submission to what?" Campbell, page 11.

Page 54: "Once having traversed the threshold, the hero moves in a dream landscape of curiously fluid, ambiguous forms, where he must survive a succession of trials. This is a favorite phase of the myth-adventure. It has produced a world literature of miraculous tests and ordeals." Campbell, page 81.

Page 178: "Not even the monastery walls . . . not even the remoteness of the desert, can defend against the female presences." Campbell, page 104.

Page 184: "Atonement (*at-one-ment*) consists in no more than the abandonment of that self-generated double monster—the dragon thought to be God (superego) and the dragon thought to be Sin (repressed id). But this requires an abandonment of the attachment to ego itself, and that is what is difficult." Campbell, pages 107 and 110.

Page 206: "In every system of theology there is an umbilical point, an Achilles tendon which the finger of the mother life has touched, and where the possibility of perfect knowledge has been impaired. The problem of the hero is to pierce himself (and therewith his world) precisely through that point; to shatter and annihilate that key knot of his limited existence." Campbell, pages 124–25.

Page 212: "If the hero in his triumph wins the blessing of the goddess or the god and then is explicitly commissioned to return to the world with some elixir for the restoration of society, the final stage of his adventure is supported by all the powers of his supernatural patron." Campbell, page 170.

Page 216: "The adventure of the hero represents the moment in his life when he achieved illumination—-the nuclear moment when, while still alive, he found and opened the road to the light beyond the dark walls of our living death." Campbell, page 222.

Page 225: "For now it appears that the perilous journey was a labor not of attainment but of reattainment, not discovery but rediscovery. The godly powers sought and dangerously won are revealed to have been within the heart of the hero all the time." Campbell, pages 30–31.

Page 226: "What, now, is the result of the miraculous passage and return?" Campbell, page 205.

Page 228: "The hero is the champion of things becoming, not of things become, because he is." Campbell, page 209.

About the Author

Nicole Chaison's Hausfrau is the title character in her triannually published *Hausfrau muthah-zine*, which chronicles the roller coaster of passion that is parenting. A one-woman show based on her stories—also called *The Passion of the Hausfrau*—opened in March 2009 at the Portland Stage Company. Chaison lives with her husband and two children in Portland, Maine.

www.passionofthehausfrau.com